Happiness, Wellbeing and Society

As Singapore continues to grow as a nation, the happiness and wellbeing of Singaporeans and what matters to them also change. This book conceptualizes and measures the cognitive and affective aspects of subjective wellbeing from multiple perspectives and relates these to important factors such as values, trust, democratic rights, views about politics and the role of the government. Through nationwide surveys using representative samples, including insights from the most recent 2016 Quality of Life (QOL) Survey, this book examines how happiness and subjective wellbeing have evolved over the past 20 years in Singapore.

This book is an invaluable resource for those interested in how the study of happiness and wellbeing in Singapore connects with and contributes to the ongoing research and discourse on happiness and wellbeing around the world.

Siok Kuan Tambyah is Associate Professor at the NUS Business School, National University of Singapore. Her research interests include consumption and identity, ethnicity, gender, luxury consumption, consumer culture, values and lifestyles, and cross-cultural consumer behavior. In addition to journal articles on consumer behavior, services marketing and quality of life, she has co-authored three books on values, lifestyles and wellbeing in Singapore.

Soo Jiuan Tan is Associate Professor at the NUS Business School, National University of Singapore. Her research is in the areas of international market entry strategies, consumer values and lifestyles, parallel importing, game theoretic applications in marketing and new product management. She has published in leading international journals and is also the co-author of five books: *Seven Faces of Singaporeans*, *Competing for Markets: Growth Strategies for SMEs*, *Understanding Singaporeans: Values, Lifestyles, Aspirations and Consumption Behaviors*, *The Wellbeing of Singaporeans*, and *Happiness and Wellbeing: The Singaporean Experience*.

Routledge Advances in Management and Business Studies

For more information about this series, please visit www.routledge.com/series/ SE0305

Happiness, Wellbeing and Society

What Matters for Singaporeans

Siok Kuan Tambyah
and Soo Jiuan Tan

Routledge
Taylor & Francis Group

LONDON AND NEW YORK

First published 2018
by Routledge
2 Park Square, Milton Park, Abingdon, Oxon OX14 4RN

and by Routledge
605 Third Avenue, New York, NY 10017

First issued in paperback 2020

Routledge is an imprint of the Taylor & Francis Group, an informa business

British Library Cataloguing-in-Publication Data
A catalogue record for this book is available from the British Library

Library of Congress Cataloging-in-Publication Data
A catalog record for this book has been requested

ISBN 13: 978-0-367-50413-7 (pbk)
ISBN 13: 978-0-815-36557-0 (hbk)

Typeset in Galliard
by Apex CoVantage, LLC

Contents

Figures

Tables

Acknowledgements

We are grateful to the National University of Singapore for its generous funding of the 2016 Quality of Life (QOL) Survey that provided the dataset for this book. We would like to thank the 1503 Singaporeans who kindly responded to this survey and shared their views on the various aspects of happiness and wellbeing. We also appreciate Jasper Teow Hong Jun for his help in the literature review related to the drafting of the survey questionnaire, Ethan Samuel Koh for his help in the data analyses, and Pritish Bhattacharya for his comments and suggestions on the income and happiness chapter.

As we publish the fifth book in the continuing research on happiness and wellbeing in Singapore, we would like to express our deepest gratitude to Professor Kau Ah Keng (1946–2015), former head of the Marketing Department at the National University of Singapore. He was a pioneer in the research on values and lifestyles in Singapore since the late 1980s and the lead researcher for the quality of life surveys conducted in 1996 and 2001.

1   Introduction, context and research methodology

This book is part of the continuing research on quality of life issues conducted by its authors and builds on past surveys on the wellbeing of Singaporeans conducted in 1996, 2001 and 2011. It focuses on the wellbeing of Singaporeans and details the findings of a large-scale survey of 1503 citizens conducted from October 2016 to February 2017. This comprehensive study provides insights into Singaporeans' satisfaction with life and living in Singapore, happiness, enjoyment, achievement, control, purpose, psychological wellbeing, economic wellbeing, overall wellbeing, personal values, value orientations, spirituality, trust, national identity, views about society and politics, democratic rights and the role of the government. Insights into most of these aspects on the wellbeing of Singaporeans will be presented in this book. In addition, this 2016 Quality of Life (QOL) Survey builds on previous studies that were done in 1996, 2001 and 2011, thus providing a longitudinal perspective into how the various aspects of the wellbeing of Singaporeans have evolved through the years.

In the sections to follow, we first provide some background information relating to Singapore's demographic, economic and political development, as well as its global connections. This provides readers, both new to and familiar with Singapore, some insights into the context in which the survey was conducted. The 2016 and/or 2017 statistics were retrieved from various websites and databases as noted in the references. Where available, we provide comparisons to statistics retrieved in 2011 and/or 2012, when the last 2011 QOL Survey was conducted.

We then discuss our rationale for conducting the QOL Surveys in Singapore, taking into account the sustained interest in wellbeing research in many parts of the world. Finally, we outline the research methodology for the 2016 QOL Survey, including the questionnaire development, sampling procedures, data quality control, the profile of respondents, representativeness of the sample and data analyses.

Singapore as a place to live

Singapore is an island city-state located at the southern tip of the Malay Peninsula. It enjoys a tropical rainforest climate, with temperatures ranging from 22° to

34° Celsius throughout the year. Although Singapore consists of 63 islands, it has a total land area of only about 700 square kilometers. Singapore was a fishing village before it was colonized by the British East India Company in 1819 and then used as a trading outpost. The island was occupied by the Japanese Empire during World War II but reverted to British rule in 1945. It joined the Malaysian Federation in 1963 and became independent in 1965. Singapore is a republic with a democratic system of unicameral parliamentary government. Most of Singapore's laws are inherited from British and British-Indian laws.

Singapore is considered one of the best places to live in Asia, if not the world. Various surveys of quality of life have placed Singapore favorably when compared to many cities in the world. The 2017 Worldwide Quality of Living Survey conducted by Mercer Human Resource Consultancy assessed Singapore to be the 25th best city in the world, one step up from the 26th spot in 2016. Incidentally, Singapore held this same position in 2011. This survey placed Singapore ahead of Tokyo's 47th position. Both cities were considered to have the highest quality of life in Asia (excluding Australian cities). The ranking by Mercer is premised upon their evaluation of the living environment in 420 cities. These quality of life assessments include the political, social, economic and sociocultural environment, health and sanitation, and other aspects such as school and education, public services and transportation, recreation, consumer goods, housing and natural environment.

Demographics and human development

Singapore is a multiethnic, multireligious and multilingual society. As at the end of June 2016, according to the Singapore Department of Statistics website, the resident population of Singaporeans and Permanent Residents consisted of Chinese as the dominant ethnic group (74.3 percent), followed by Malays (13.4 percent), Indians (9.1 percent) and Others (3.2 percent). There are considerable freedom and plurality in the practice of religions such as Buddhism, Christianity, Islam, Hinduism, and so on. The national language is Malay, but the other official languages of English, Mandarin and Tamil are widely spoken by the population.

In 2017, the population in Singapore was estimated to be 5.676 million (an increase from 5.18 million in 2011), of which 3.96 million were residents (3.79 million in 2011). Based on 2017 figures from the Singapore Department of Statistics website, the life expectancy at birth was recorded to be 82.9 years (81.8 years in 2011), with males averaging 80.6 years (79.3 years in 2011) and females 85.1 years (84.1 years in 2011). The literacy rate in 2016 among residents aged 15 years and above was around 97 percent (96 percent in 2011), with 52.8 percent of resident nonstudents aged 25 years and above possessing at least a postsecondary school education. Home ownership was rather high among residents and recorded to be around 90.9 percent. Singapore is a relatively safe place, with a crime rate of about 588 per 100,000 (606 per 100,000 in 2011).

The Human Development Index (HDI) looks at happiness not just from an economic perspective but also with respect to health and education. The index comprises three components: national income, life expectancy and literacy. In 2010, three new measures were added: inequality-adjusted HDI, the Gender Inequality Index and the Multidimensional Poverty Index. In 2016, a total of 188 countries were included in the HDI rankings. The HDI classifies countries into one of three clusters according to their human development attainment. Singapore was joint fifth with Denmark in 2017 (26th in 2011), with a score of 0.925 (0.866 in 2011). Singapore is in the very high human development cluster and more highly ranked than Hong Kong (12th), Japan (17th), South Korea (18th) and Brunei (30th). No figures were available for Taiwan as it has been excluded from membership in the United Nations. Malaysia (59th) is in the high human development cluster, while most of the other South East Asian countries are in the medium human development cluster. Myanmar (145th) is in the low human development cluster. Singapore has usually done well on the HDI because of its strong economic performance (GDP) and the favorable statistics about life expectancy and literacy.

Economic development, governance and stability

Since independence, the current ruling party, the People's Action Party, has been in power. This political stability, coupled with an effective government and administration, has contributed to the economic development of the country from primarily a trading port to a global city hub. Singapore's development was based on a market-driven economic system, with an emphasis on industrialization and export orientation.

According to the Singapore Department of Statistics and figures released in 2016, the economy grew at 2.0 percent (4.9 percent in 2011) and the per capita GDP was reported to be S$73,167 (S$63,050 in 2011). The average monthly household income in 2016 was S$10,336, up from S$8722 in 2011, S$6181 in 2006 and S$5972 in 2001. Inflationary pressures for the last few years (5.2 percent inflation rate in 2011) eased in 2016 (inflation rate of –0.5 percent) and 2017 (inflation rate of 0.4 percent). The unemployment rate in 2017 was low at 2.1 percent (similar to 2011). The Ministry of Manpower noted that over the last ten years, from 2007 to 2017, the average number of paid hours worked per week remained relatively constant at around 45 to 46 hours.

In the 2017 Index of Economic Freedom published by the Heritage Foundation, which ranks 186 nations in terms of their levels of economic freedom, Singapore was assessed as 88.6 percent free (87.5 percent free in 2012), making it the world's second freest economy after Hong Kong. The assessment of economic freedom was based on 12 measures along four dimensions as follows: rule of law, government size, regulatory efficiency and open markets. Singapore performed well in property rights (97.1), business freedom (95.1), judicial effectiveness (91.5) and labor freedom (90.8).

According to surveys examined by Transparency International and the Corruption Perceptions Index that they computed, Singapore was perceived to have the least corrupt public sector among Asian nations in 2016 and was also ranked at 7th (5th in 2011) on a global scale of 176 countries with a score of 8.4 (9.2 in 2011). The countries ranked ahead of Singapore were New Zealand and Denmark (joint 1st), Finland (3rd), Sweden (4th), Switzerland (5th) and Norway (6th). The 2016 report on Corruption in Asia by Political and Economic Risk Consultancy (PERC) Ltd. rated Singapore's government as having the highest level of integrity in Asia, Australia and United States. Its level of corruption had a score of 1.67, followed by Australia (2.67), Japan (3.0), Hong Kong (3.40) and the United States (4.61).

The Worldwide Cost of Living Report from The Economist Intelligence Unit (EIU) is a biannual survey that compares more than 400 individual prices across 160 products and services. Singapore topped the ranks as the most expensive city to live in for 2017 (the fourth consecutive year). Although costs of living were high in Singapore, there were some areas of relative value compared to its regional peers, for categories such as personal care, household goods and domestic help. Singapore still remained the most expensive city in the world to buy and run a car and the second-priciest city in which to purchase clothes. In terms of liveability, Singapore was doing relatively well (ranked 46th and 35th in 2016 and 2017 respectively) according to the EIU Global Liveability Rankings. The EIU ranks cities by assigning each a rating for over 30 qualitative and quantitative factors across five broad categories (such as stability, healthcare, culture and environment, education, and infrastructure). The ratings are then compiled and weighted to give a score out of 100. Along with Amsterdam, Reykjavik, Budapest and Montevideo, Singapore has seen an improvement in its liveability ranks for the past year. This was due largely to the relative stability within the countries these cities were located in.

Political rights and civil liberties

Although Singapore is ranked highly in terms of economic freedom, political freedom is less favorably assessed. In the 2017 report published by the international NGO Freedom House, Singapore was described as "partly free," having a score of 4 on both civil liberties and political rights. A rating of 1 suggests the highest degree of freedom and 7 the least amount of freedom. In East Asia, the only four "free" nations are Taiwan, Mongolia, Japan and South Korea.

Global connections

The KOF Globalization Index uses three indicators for its rankings: economic globalization, social globalization and political globalization. For 2017, Singapore was the 20th (18th in 2011) most globalized nation overall. For economic globalization, Singapore was given the top spot in a field of 187 countries (97.77 points). This means that Singapore was the most economically globalized in terms of the extent of cross-border trade, investment and revenue flows in relation to GDP, and the impact of restrictions on trade and capital transactions. Singapore also came in first (91.61 points) in terms of social globalization. This was measured along dimensions such as (a) cross-border personal contexts in the form of telephone calls, letters, and tourist flows, (b) the size of the resident foreign population, (c) cross-border information flows, such as access to the Internet, TV and foreign press products, and (d) cultural proximity to the global mainstream. In sharp contrast, for political globalization, Singapore came in at the 134th position (77th in 2011). Political globalization for Singapore was assessed according to the number of embassies it has, its memberships in international organizations, participation in United Nations peace missions and the number of bilateral and multilateral agreements it has concluded.

Social progress

The Social Progress Index determines what it means to be a good society according to three dimensions: Basic Human Needs (food, water, shelter, safety); Foundations of Wellbeing (basic education, information, health and a sustainable environment); and Opportunity (do people have rights, freedom of choice, freedom from discrimination, and access to higher education?). These 12 components form the Social Progress framework. Singapore was unranked on the 2017 Social Progress Index due to insufficient data for the Basic Humans Needs dimension. However, its scorecard indicated top-ranked positions for GDP (gross domestic product) PPP (purchasing power parity) per capita and two aspects of the Basic Human Needs dimension (Water and Sanitation, and Shelter). Singapore was also ranked 3rd for Personal Safety (also Basic Human Needs) and 4th for Health and Wellness (Foundations of Wellbeing).

The 2017 Social Progress Index findings revealed that countries achieved widely divergent levels of social progress, even at similar levels of GDP per capita. For example, a country with high GDP per capita may do well on absolute social progress, reflecting high income, yet underperform relative to countries of similar income. Singapore has a similar GDP per capita to those of countries like Norway, Switzerland, United States, Ireland, Saudi Arabia, Netherlands, Austria, Sweden, Denmark, Germany, Australia, Canada, Belgium, Iceland and Finland. However, compared to these countries, Singapore underperformed in the areas of Access to Basic Knowledge, and Access to Information and Communications (Foundations of Wellbeing), Personal Rights, and Tolerance and Inclusion (Opportunity).

Rationale for the QOL Surveys in Singapore

Research on wellbeing has been ongoing for many years around the world. Many varied concerns about wellbeing ranging from the economics of happiness to the eudaimonics of happiness have been addressed in academic circles, as well as in the policy-making arena. Researchers involved in wellbeing research have noted the limitations in using GNP (gross national product) and GDP as a measurement for or indicator of the quality of life because other aspects of wellbeing cannot be adequately accounted for with economic prosperity. We also recognize these limitations in a relatively wealthy country like Singapore and the need for a more holistic perspective of wellbeing.

As recommended in the Report by the Commission on the Measurement of Economic Performance and Social Progress, "[M]easures of subjective wellbeing provide key information about people's quality of life. Statistical offices should incorporate questions to capture people's life evaluations, hedonic experiences and priorities in their own surveys" (p. 58). Currently, many well regarded worldwide surveys and indexes are administered by various national agencies and governments, international agencies (e.g., the Better Life Initiative by the Organisation for Economic Co-operation and Development [OECD], the World Happiness Report by the United Nations, etc.) and research institutes. Singapore has been a part of some worldwide surveys, notably the Gallup World Poll and the World Values Survey.

Some organizations collect their primary data through carefully crafted surveys, while others collate publicly available secondary data and then repackage and present the data in line with their own research agenda and aims. These surveys and indexes provide some form of comparative analyses across countries and regions. The usefulness of such analyses depends on many factors, including the completeness, accuracy and integrity of the data collated and the algorithms used in calculating the indexes. To facilitate comparative analyses, the surveys usually rely on common measures of subjective wellbeing. Some of these measures are established and validated scales related to happiness, enjoyment and satisfaction with life. While these common measures are beneficial in some way, it would be useful to have context-specific measures of subjective wellbeing to account for the unique characteristics of certain countries and to provide more in-depth insights.

Many countries and regions have their own versions of a quality of life and wellbeing survey that is focused on their particularistic needs and contexts (e.g., the European Social Survey). One of the forerunners is Bhutan, which instituted its own Gross Happiness Index with unique indicators such as Community Vitality, Cultural Diversity and Resilience, Time Use, and Ecological Diversity and Resilience. Some of these surveys and indexes are administered by government agencies, while others are from independently funded research agencies. For the Singaporean context, we have developed the QOL Surveys, which incorporate both common measures (more for comparison across countries) and context-specific measures (more for comparison across years within the country). Some of these context-specific measures are related to value orientations, satisfaction with life domains and satisfaction with living in Singapore. We have tried to collect data on the wellbeing of Singaporeans every five years since 1996. The QOL Surveys we conduct in Singapore provide us with an opportunity to obtain the indicators of subjective wellbeing that are relevant to Singaporeans and to support our analyses and interpretation when comparing our data with other research studies.

In addition to surveys to measure perceptions of subjective wellbeing and the development of indexes, many countries have incorporated happiness as part of their national goals. On July 19, 2011, the United Nations General Assembly formally approved a Bhutan-sponsored resolution (65/309) entitled "Happiness: Towards a Holistic Approach to Development." In doing so, the Assembly formally recognized the pursuit of happiness as a fundamental human goal. From 2012, the United Nations had shared the World Happiness Report (comprising a suite of wellbeing measures and indicators) to monitor and compare levels and sources of happiness of its member countries on an annual basis.

In reciting Singapore's pledge, the citizens of Singapore commit themselves to being one united people and to build a democratic society to achieve happiness, prosperity and progress for the nation. It is imperative that those concerned about the wellbeing of Singaporeans, citizens, researchers and policy makers alike, consider the far-reaching implications of this pledge and its impact on Singaporean society. In our role as researchers, we have conducted various QOL Surveys and provided insights into what matters for Singaporeans in terms of their happiness and wellbeing. These insights have been shared at conferences and in books, book chapters and journal articles.

Research methodology

A person's sense of wellbeing incorporates feelings of fulfillment, joy, happiness, pleasure and satisfaction. Objective indicators alone are not sufficient for a meaningful assessment of the quality of life. Subjective indicators are needed as people evaluate their life experiences according to their own values and beliefs about what is good and right in life, that is, through their own evaluations of what they experience. The 2016 QOL Survey (like its predecessors) relies mainly on subjective indicators (evaluations and perceptions). We also collect information on the demographic background of the respondents.

Questionnaire development

As mentioned, the 2016 QOL Survey is part of an ongoing stream of research on the wellbeing of Singaporeans, using nationwide surveys and representative samples. Previous surveys were conducted in 1996, 2001 and 2011. Based on a review of recent research on wellbeing and feedback from the 1996, 2001 and 2011 surveys, we discussed what to include in the 2016 QOL Survey. For instance, questions on work and family, as well as Schwartz's Higher Order Values (Schwartz 2007), were added to the questionnaire for the 2016 QOL Survey. To facilitate longitudinal comparisons, most of the key items relating to satisfaction with various aspects of life, along with the value orientations examined in the 1996, 2001, and 2011 surveys, were retained for the 2016 QOL Survey.

Like its predecessors, the 2016 QOL Survey questionnaire was first drafted in English and pretested among a small group of potential respondents. Any ambiguities or inconsistencies were eliminated based on the feedback collected. The survey questionnaire was then translated into Chinese, Malay and Tamil for respondents who were not familiar with English. This was completed by the market research firm that was tasked to conduct the fieldwork.

The format and ordering of the questions in the 2016 QOL Survey question-naire are briefly described as follows. To measure value orientations, 31 statements on attitudes and values such as family values, status consciousness, materialism, eco-orientation, volunteerism, societal consciousness, traditionalism, entrepre-neurial spirit, and e-orientation were included in Section A of the questionnaire. Respondents were required to answer each statement using a Likert scale with 1 as "strongly disagree" to 6 for "strongly agree." For Schwartz's Higher Order Values scale, respondents were required to indicate whether they were similar to the person described in each of the 21 statements, on a scale ranging from "1 = not like me at all" to "6 = very much like me."

To investigate satisfaction with life and life domains, we had three measures on satisfaction in Section B of the questionnaire. First, respondents were asked to express their degree of satisfaction with life. This was the Satisfaction with Life Scale (Diener et al. 1985) used in the European Social Values Survey. This was the first time we used this scale in our research. Second, they were asked about 15 life domains, such as household income, friendships, marriage/romantic relationships and jobs, as well as their satisfaction with the overall quality of life in general (a scale used in our 1996, 2001 and 2011 surveys). Third, they were asked to rate their degree of satisfaction with 25 aspects of life in Singapore and their satisfaction with the overall quality of life in Singapore. Opinions pertaining to satisfaction with the overall quality of life in general and the overall quality of life in Singapore were assessed using a 6-point scale with 1 being "very dissatisfied" to 6 for being "very satisfied" (a scale used in our 1996, 2001 and 2011 surveys).

For work–life balance (Section C), respondents were asked to indicate their degree of agreement with 18 statements about their work and family life, using a 6-point scale with 1 being "strongly disagree" to 6 being "strongly agree." The work–family conflict scale was adapted from Carlson et al. (2000). For psychological wellbeing in Section D, respondents were asked to rate their agreement with 12 statements on different aspects of psychological wellbeing, on a scale from "1 = strongly disagree" to "6 = strongly agree." Respondents assessed their economic wellbeing (Section E) by answering four questions relating to whether they have enough money to buy things they need, to do what they want, to make a major purchase and to meet their loan commitments. A fifth question was on the people they would turn to if they had financial difficulties. To measure overall wellbeing (Section F), we asked respondents to indicate which step they are on a ladder comprising 11 steps (0 to 10) now and where they expected to be in five years. In Section G, we adopted the List of Values developed by Kahle (1983) for our respondents to indicate the importance of each of the nine personal values listed using 1 as "not important at all" to 6 for "very important."

In Section H, we adapted three questions from the AsiaBarometer Survey for respondents to report on the state of their happiness ("1 = very unhappy" to "5 = very happy"), whether they enjoy life ("1 = never" to "4 = often") and whether they felt that they have accomplished what they want out of their life ("1 = none" to "4 = a great deal"). We adapted Tinkler and Hicks' (2011) scale on locus of control for respondents to report on how much control they have over important aspects of their life ("1 = none" to "4 = a great deal") and a sense of purpose scale for respondents to report on how much they felt they have a sense of purpose in their life ("1 = none" to "4 = a great deal").

On the issue of trust (Section J), we asked respondents three questions adopted from the ASEAN Barometer Survey (2009) to measure generalized trust (see Tan and Tambyah 2013). These questions were (1) "Generally, do you think most people can be trusted or that you can't be too careful in dealing with people?"; (2) "Do you think most people would try to take advantage of you if they got a chance, or would they try to be fair?" and (3) "Do you think that people generally try to be helpful or that they are mostly looking out for themselves?" The responses were coded on a 2-point scale: "1 = most people can be trusted," "2 = you can't be too careful in dealing with people," "1 = most people would try to be fair," "2 = most people would try to take advantage of me," "1 = people generally try to be helpful," and "2 = people mostly look out for themselves." Respondents were also asked to indicate the level of trust they have (from "1 = do not trust at all" to "4 = trust a lot") in various types of institutions in Singapore, such as the political, public service, economic, social and international institutions. We also included questions on spirituality (Section K) with questions relating to whether people believe in spirituality and religious principles ("1 = strongly disagree" to "6 = strongly agree"), as well as the extent they engage in religious practices ("1 = never" to "5 = daily").

To examine views relating to society, politics and the role of the government (Sections L and M), we asked respondents whether they agreed or disagreed with statements relating to Society and Politics (e.g., "Citizens have a right to vote") and the Role of the Government (e.g., "The government should do more to protect the environment"). In both sections, respondents indicated their responses on a scale of "1 = strongly disagree" to "5 = strongly agree." These questions were also drawn from the AsiaBarometer Surveys. Finally, the demographic questions were included in the last section of the questionnaire (Section N).

The 2016 QOL Survey questionnaire consisted of 21 pages with scale items measuring 240 variables. Generally, the survey questionnaire was comprehensive and covered many aspects of the quality of life of the respondents. However, for this book, we have selected a list of variables for in-depth analyses as shown in Table 1.1. The Value Orientations, Schwartz's Higher Order Values, List of Values, Generalized Trust, and the Society and Government variables were used as input variables in our analyses. The three Life Satisfaction concepts, and the Wellbeing Indicators of happiness, enjoyment, achievement, control, purpose, psychological flourishing and economic wellbeing were used as outcome variables. As described in the previous sections, the variables are all perceptual in nature; hence the measures obtained are subjective measurements.

Table 1.1 Variables included in the book

Input variables	Value orientations	Family values, status consciousness, materialism, volunteerism, societal consciousness, traditionalism, and entrepreneurial spirit.
	Schwartz's Higher Order Values	Conservation, openness to change, self-transcendence, and self-enhancement
	List of Values	Being well-respected, excitement, fun and enjoyment in life, security, self-fulfillment, self-respect, sense of accomplishment, sense of belonging, and warm relationships with others
	Generalized trust	Can people be trusted? Do people try to take advantage of you? Do people try to be helpful?
	Society and Government	Satisfaction with democratic rights, views about politics, and role of the government
Input/ control variables	Demographics	Of the respondent and of the household the respondent lives in
		Age, education, gender, monthly household income and marital status
Outcome variables	Life satisfaction	Satisfaction with life, 15 life domains and satisfaction with the overall quality of life in general, 25 aspects of life in Singapore and satisfaction with the overall quality of life in Singapore
	Wellbeing indicators	Happiness, enjoyment, achievement, control, purpose, psychological flourishing, and economic wellbeing

Sampling frame

The study covered a representative sample of households in Singapore according to the 2015 General Household Survey (Singapore Department of Statistics 2015). Only Singapore citizens were invited to participate in the survey. For this study, the minimum age was 15 years old. For respondents aged 15 to 17 years, verbal consent was obtained from a parent or adult prior to the data collection.

A list of 1500 household addresses were randomly selected from all residential areas across Singapore. The sampling frame provided a comprehensive reach of respondents across the Singapore population, thus ensuring data representativeness and findings that are reflective of the population.

Sampling method

Randomness of data was emphasized to ensure that the findings from the study were reflective of the population of interest. Systematic random sampling was employed, first in the selection of household, followed by the selection of respondent. This sampling procedure ensured that there was minimal self-selection bias for age, occupation, race and housing types.

Fieldwork

Fifteen interviewers were actively deployed for this study at any one time. Interviewers from the three major ethnic groups, that is Chinese, Malay and Indian, were recruited for this study. Trained interviewers were sent to the specified zones to conduct the surveys. The fieldwork was carried out over a period of 12 weeks, from October 28, 2016 to February 5, 2017. Respondents for the survey were given a S$20 voucher as a token of appreciation. To prevent bias, the token was given only after the survey was completed.

Data quality control

To ensure that good-quality data had been collected, quality control steps were taken at different stages of the research process. At the pre-data collection stage, additional pretests of the questionnaire were conducted, and changes were made to ensure that respondents understood the questions in the survey. Surveyors recruited for the fieldwork were also trained.

At the data collection stage, every survey submitted was checked thoroughly by the fieldwork manager for face validity and consistency. Error cases were flagged, and the respondent was contacted by phone for verification where a contact number was available. To allow sufficient time for appropriate corrective actions, surveys were checked daily by the fieldwork manager. Stringent in-house callbacks were conducted to verify surveys and to double-check answers. Call-backs were conducted on a minimum of 50 percent of surveyor returns for their initial batch and a minimum of 30 percent for subsequent batches. This stringent check was much higher than the industry average norm of 10 percent to 30 percent.

At the preanalysis stage, a minimum of 10 percent random checks were conducted against the data entered to ensure data entry accuracy. After the data was entered and physical checks completed, another round of checks was done using SPSS on the database. For instance, range checks were run to make sure that all answers given were within the range specified in the questionnaire. Respondents were contacted to clarify any inconsistencies found in the responses. All doubtful cases that were unfit for analysis were voided before the final database was verified ready for analysis.

The profile of respondents

The demographic background of the respondents in this study is presented in Table 1.2. As indicated, the gender balance was about equal. Close to two-thirds (60.9 percent) of the respondents were married, and 81.7 percent of the respondents were below 65 years of age. Chinese respondents accounted for almost 77 percent of the total number interviewed, with 14.5 percent of Malays, 7.3 percent of Indians and the remaining (1.2 percent) from other ethnic groups.

Table 1.2 Profile of respondents

2016 QOL Survey	%	N
1. Gender		
• Male	48.6	731
• Female	51.4	772
Total	100.0	1503
2. Marital status		
• Single	33.0	54
• Married	67.0	922
Total	100.0	1376
3. Age (years)		
• 15–19	7.4	111
• 20–24	7.7	115
• 25–29	8.4	127
• 30–34	8.1	122
• 35–39	9.9	149
• 40–44	9.8	148
• 45–49	9.0	136
• 50–54	10.1	152
• 55–59	8.6	130
• 60–64	7.3	110
• 65–70	5.6	84
• 70–74	3.7	56
• 75–79	2.9	44
• 80 and above	1.3	19
Total	100.0	1503
4. Education		
• Primary school and below	14.6	220
• Secondary/ITE	33.5	503
• GCE A/diploma	24.3	365
• University	22.0	330
• Postgraduate	5.7	85
Total	100.0	1503
5. Household income (monthly)		
• S$1000 or below	7.8	117
• S$1001–S$2000	7.4	111
• S$2001–S$3000	8.4	126
• S$3001–S$4000	6.0	90
• S$4001–S$5000	5.4	81
• S$5001–S$6000	4.9	74

2016 QOL Survey	%	N
• S$6001–S$7000	2.8	42
• S$7001–S$8000	3.3	50
• S$8001–S$9000	2.3	34
• S$9001–S$10,000	2.7	41
• S$10,001–S$12,000	3.8	57
• S$12,001–S$15,000	2.7	41
• S$15,001–S$20,000	2.4	36
• More than S$20,000	2.7	41
• Refused	37.4	562
Total	100.0	1503
6. Religion		
• Buddhism	32.0	481
• Christianity	14.2	214
• Catholicism	4.8	72
• Hinduism	5.1	77
• Sikhism	.4	6
• Islam	16.2	244
• Taoism	8.0	120
• Other religions	.4	6
• No religion	18.8	283
Total	100.0	1503
7. Race		
• Chinese	76.2	1146
• Malay	14.0	210
• Indian	7.9	118
• Others	1.9	29
Total	100.0	1503

Respondents also had different educational levels, ranging from those with primary education or below (17.8 percent) to those with tertiary education and higher (25.9 percent). For household incomes, 562 respondents declined to answer this question, leaving a sample of 941 respondents. For the data analysis, we divided the respondents into four income brackets, and there were sufficient numbers for each income bracket as follows: 354 (low – S$3000 or less), 337 (medium-low – S$3001 to S$8000), 173 (medium-high – S$8001 to S$15,000) and 77 (high – those earning S$15,001 and more). The rationale will be discussed later in the Data Analyses section.

Representativeness of sample

The representativeness of the sample was examined by comparing certain important demographic characteristics with those of the population at large and the Singapore citizen population. The variables examined included gender, age and race. The demographic characteristics of the sample and those of the total Singapore population were very similar. There was a good balance of males and females in the sample, and the distribution was very close to that of the total population. The age distributions of the sample and Singapore's total population were also very similar, with very small underrepresentation (0.1 percent) of the 30- to39-year age group (17.9 percent for total Singapore population versus 18 percent for our sample) and the 70-year and above age group (8.4 percent for total Singapore population versus 7.9 percent for our sample). In terms of race, the distributions of the sample and the total population were fairly close. The Chinese and the Malays were slightly overrepresented by 1.9 percent (74.3 percent for total Singapore population versus 76.2 percent for our sample) and 0.7 percent (13.3 percent for total Singapore population versus 14 percent for our sample), respectively, while the Indians and Others were underrepresented by 1.2 percent (9.1 percent for total Singapore population versus 7.9 percent for our sample) and 2.1 percent (3.3 percent for total Singapore population versus 1.2 percent for our sample), respectively.

Since our survey was for Singapore citizens only, the representativeness of the sample was also examined by comparing the same demographic characteristics with those of the Singapore citizen population. There was a good balance of males and females in the sample, and the distribution was very close to that of the Singapore citizen population. The age distributions of the sample and the Singapore citizen population were quite close, although the sample appeared to have a slight overrepresentation (2.9 percent) of the 30- to 39-year age group (15.1 percent for Singapore citizen population versus 18 percent for our sample). There were also a slight underrepresentation (1.3 percent) of the 60- to 69-year age group (14.2 percent for the Singapore citizen population versus 12.9 percent for our sample) and a slight underrepresentation (1.5 percent) for the 70-year and above age group (9.4 percent for Singapore citizen population versus 7.9 percent for our sample). In terms of race, the distributions of the sample and the Singapore citizen population were also quite close. Malays were slightly overrepresented by 1.6 percent (12.4 percent for the Singapore citizen population versus 14 percent for our sample), while the Indians and Others were very slightly underrepresented by 1.3 percent (9.2 percent for Singapore citizen population versus 7.9 percent for our sample) and 0.7 percent (1.9 percent for the Singapore citizen population versus 1.2 percent for our sample), respectively.

In view of the slight over- and underrepresentations, we weighted the data according to data on Singapore Citizens from the General Household Survey 2015 (Singapore Department of Statistics 2015) to make the sample data representative of the Singapore citizen population. Key dimensions of the Singapore citizen population in terms of age, gender and race were used to weight the survey sample data. The demographic profiles (for the weighted and unweighted datasets) are summarized in Table 1.3.

We also conducted a series of data analyses such as frequency distribution, cross-tabulation and computation of mean scores using the original and weighted samples to see whether there were any significant deviations in the responses due to the slight over- and underrepresentations. Our analyses revealed insignificant differences in the results derived from both sets of samples.

As the characteristics of the sample were generally close to that of the total population and the Singapore citizen population, and the differences in responses between the original and the weighted data were insignificant, the data was deemed representative and would subsequently be analyzed without using the weights.

Table 1.3 Breakdown of sample respondents by age, gender and race for weighted and unweighted datasets

Demographics	Unweighted dataset of respondents		Weighted dataset of respondents	Singapore citizens (General Household Survey 2015)
Breakdown of sample respondents by age				
Age	N	%	%	%
15–19	111	7.4	7.1	7.8
20–29	242	16.1	16.2	16.6
30–39	271	18.0	14.8	15.1
40–49	284	18.9	16.2	17.3
50–59	282	18.8	18.7	19.6
60–69	194	12.9	15.5	14.2
70 and above	119	7.9	11.4	9.4
Total	1503	100.0	100.0	100.0
Breakdown of sample respondents by gender				
Gender	N	%	%	%
Male	731	48.6	48.3	49.7
Female	772	51.4	51.7	50.3
Total	1503	100.0	100.0	100.0
Breakdown of sample respondents by race				
Race	N	%	%	%
Chinese	1146	76.2	76.9	76.2
Malay	210	14.0	14.5	15.0
Indian	118	7.9	7.3	7.4
Others	29	1.9	1.2	1.4
Total	1503	100.0	100.0	100.0

Data analyses

In the following chapters, descriptive analyses involving frequency tabulations, means comparisons, cross-tabulations and the construction of indexes will be presented for the data collected. In addition, we conducted correlation analyses to examine the relationships among the variables investigated, regression analyses to examine the impact of input variables (e.g., personal values, trust and views about politics) on life satisfaction and the wellbeing indicators, and clustering analysis to differentiate the various types of Singaporeans.

We also tested for individual differences among demographic groups using age, education, gender, monthly household income, and marital status. Race was not used for analysis due to the very small number of respondents in two out of the four racial groups in Singapore. This was also the case in our past QOL studies (1996, 2001 and 2011). For education, we have three levels: low (those with no formal education or primary school education), medium (those with secondary/GCE O Level, postsecondary/ITE or GCE A Level/Diploma qualifications) and high (those with university or postgraduate degrees). For monthly household incomes, we have four income levels: low (those earning S$3000 or less), medium-low (those earning S$3001 to S$8000), medium-high (those earning S$8001 to S$15,000) and high (those earning S$15,001 and more). These levels were decided based on statistics from the General Household Survey 2015 (Singapore Department of Statistics 2015). The median household income from work was S$8666 (Singapore Department of Statistics 2015), and the income ceiling to qualify for public housing (executive condominium) was S$15,000. For marital status, we compared the responses of single and married people as the numbers for those who are divorced, widowed or separated were too small.

Overview of book chapters

Within each chapter, we first provide some theoretical background for the concepts and issues to be discussed by outlining relevant research studies and literature. We then detail the data analyses and findings of the 2016 QOL Survey, with comparison to our previous surveys in Singapore and other research studies where applicable.

In Chapter 2, we analyze the cognitive aspects of subjective wellbeing by looking at the satisfaction of Singaporeans with regard to various life domains and aspects of living in Singapore. Sources of individual differences among demographic groups are also discussed. For the 2016 QOL Survey, we report the results on the Satisfaction with Life Scale, which is regularly used in other surveys such as the European Social Values Survey.

In Chapter 3, we focus on the more affective aspects of subjective wellbeing and report on Singaporeans' level of happiness, enjoyment, achievement, control, purpose and psychological flourishing. We also discuss sources of individual differences across demographic groups.

In Chapter 4, we investigate whether money can buy happiness in Singapore by looking for inflexion points in wellbeing indicators like happiness, enjoyment, achievement, control, purpose, satisfaction with life, satisfaction with the overall quality of life and satisfaction with the overall quality of life in Singapore across different income groups. We discuss the measure of economic wellbeing in terms of four questions (three were adopted from the Gallup–Healthways Well-Being Index), on whether one has enough money to buy the things one needs, to fulfil monthly loan commitments, to do things one wants to do, and to carry out a major financial transaction.

In Chapter 5, we use the List of Values and Schwartz's Higher Order Values to assess the importance of certain personal values to all Singaporeans and specific demographic groups. Besides tracking changes in the List of Values over time, we also conduct regression analyses to examine the impact of the List of Values and Schwartz's Higher Order Values on Singaporeans' subjective wellbeing.

In Chapter 6, we discuss the value orientations of Singaporeans such as family values, eco-orientation, status consciousness, volunteerism, traditionalism, entre-preneurial spirit and materialism. We also use clustering analysis to define groups of Singaporeans based on these value orientations. Comparisons among the clusters of 2001, 2011 and 2016 provide interesting insights on how the value orientations of Singaporeans have evolved.

In Chapter 7, we examine Singaporeans' level and variation of generalized trust and provide comparative analyses as to whether certain demographic seg-ments are more trusting than others. We also discuss how generalized trust as a form of social capital has an impact on wellbeing (i.e., happiness, health and life satisfaction).

In Chapter 8, we first examine Singaporeans' satisfaction with their rights as citizens and their views on various aspects of politics. We then discuss Singa-poreans' views on the role of the government and areas where they feel the government should allocate more resources. We also show how these perceptions vary across demographic groups and how they may influence the wellbeing of Singaporeans (i.e., overall quality of life in Singapore).

In Chapter 9, we conclude with an overview of the key findings of the QOL 2016 Survey and how the QOL Surveys in Singapore provide unique insights into the research on happiness and wellbeing. We also propose directives for future research in these areas.

References

Asia Barometer Survey. www.asiabarometer.org (accessed January 6, 2018).

Bhutan's Gross National Happiness Index. www.grossnationalhappiness.com/ (accessed November 22, 2017).

Carlson, D., Kacmar, M., and Williams, L. (2000), 'Construction and initial valida-tion of a multidimensional measure of work-family conflict', *Journal of Vocational Behavior*, 56(2), 249–276.

Commission on the Measurement of Economic Performance and Social Progress. http://citeseerx.ist.psu.edu/viewdoc/download?doi=10.1.1.215.58&rep=rep1&type=pdf (accessed November 22, 2017).

Diener, E., Emmons, R.A., Larsen, R.J., and Griffin, S. (1985), 'The satisfaction with life scale', *Journal of Personality Assessment*, 49, 71–75.

Economist Intelligence Unit Democracy Index 2016. www.eiu.com/public/thankyou_download.aspx?activity=download&campaignid=DemocracyIndex2016 www.eiu.com/public/topical_report.aspx?campaignid=DemocracyIndex2016 (all accessed November 7, 2017).

Economist Intelligence Unit Global Liveability Ranking Report 2017. www.eiu.com/public/thankyou_download.aspx?activity=download&campaignid=Liveability17 (accessed November 7, 2017).

Economist Intelligence Unit Worldwide Cost of Living Report 2017. www.eiu.com/Handlers/WhitepaperHandler.ashx?fi=WCOL_Summary_Whitepaper_2017.pdf&mode=wp&campaignid=WCOL2017 (accessed November 7, 2017).

Freedom House. https://freedomhouse.org/blog/china-and-singapore-models-not-follow https://freedomhouse.org/blog/singapore-and-limits-authoritarian-prosperity https://freedomhouse.org/report/fiw-2017-table-country-scores (all accessed November 7, 2017). https://freedomhouse.org/report/freedom-world/freedom-world-2017 (accessed 22 January 2018).

Gallup World Poll. www.gallup.de/182702/gallup-world-poll.aspx (accessed December 4, 2017).

Human Development Index. http://hdr.undp.org/en/content/human-development-index-hdi http://hdr.undp.org/sites/default/files/HDR2016_EN_Overview_Web.pdf http://hdr.undp.org/sites/default/files/2016_human_development_report.pdf (all accessed November 7, 2017).

Index of Economic Freedom. www.heritage.org/index/country/singapore (accessed November 7, 2017).

Kahle, L.R. (1983), *Social values and social change: Adaptation to life in America*, New York, NY, USA: Praeger.

KOF Globalization Index. http://globalization.kof.ethz.ch/ www.statista.com/statistics/268168/globalization-index-by-country/ www.statista.com/statistics/268171/index-of-economic-globalization/ www.statista.com/statistics/268170/index-of-social-globalization/ www.statista.com/statistics/268169/index-for-political-globalization/ Press Release: http://globalization.kof.ethz.ch/media/filer_public/2017/04/19/press_release_2017_en.pdf (all accessed November 7, 2017).

Mercer Human Resource Consultancy-Worldwide Quality of Living Survey. www.mercer.com/newsroom/2017-quality-of-living-survey.html https://mobilityexchange.mercer.com/Portals/0/Content/Rankings/rankings/qol2017e784512/index.html (all accessed November 7, 2017).

Ministry of Manpower. Paid Hours Worked: http://stats.mom.gov.sg/Pages/Hours-Worked-Summary-Table.aspx (accessed November 7, 2017).

Organisation for Economic Co-operation and Development (OECD). http://www.oecd.org/statistics/better-life-initiative.htm (accessed December 4, 2017).

Political and Economic Risk Consultancy Ltd. (PERC). http://asiarisk.com/subscribe/exsum1.pdf (accessed November 7, 2017).

Schwartz, S.H. (2007), 'Value orientations: Measurement, antecedents and consequences across nations', in *Measuring attitudes cross-nationally: Lessons from the*

European Social Survey, edited by R. Jowell, C. Roberts, R. Fitzgerald and G. Eva, London, UK: Sage, 169–203.

Singapore Department of Statistics. Household Income: www.singstat.gov.sg/statistics/browse-by-theme/household-income-tables (accessed November 7, 2017). Singapore General Household Survey: www.singstat.gov.sg/publications/publications-and-papers/GHS/ghs2015 (accessed November 7, 2017). www.singstat.gov.sg/docs/default-source/default-document- Racial Composition of Population: library/publications/publications_and_papers/population_and_population_structure/population2016.pdf (accessed November 11, 2017). Life Expectancy: www.singstat.gov.sg/statistics/visualising-data/charts/life-expectancy-at-birth (accessed December 4, 2017).

Singapore's Pledge. https://www.nhb.gov.sg/what-we-do/our-work/community-engagement/education/resources/national-symbols/national-pledge (accessed November 22, 2017).

Social Progress Index. www.socialprogressindex.com/assets/downloads/resources/en/English-2017-Social-Progress-Index-Findings-Report_embargo-d-until-June-21-2017.pdf (accessed November 22, 2017). Singapore's Scorecard: www.socialprogressindex.com/?tab=2&code=SGP (accessed November 22, 2017).

Tan, S.J. and Tambyah, S.K. (2013), 'Trusting propensity and trust in institutions: A comparative study of 5 ASEAN nations', in *Psychology of trust: New research*, edited by D. Gefen, New York, NY, USA: Nova Science, 281–304.

Tinkler, L. and Hicks, S. (2011), *Measuring subjective well-being*. London, UK: Office for National Statistics.

Transparency International. Corruption in the Asia Pacific Region. www.transparency.org/news/feature/corruption_perceptions_index_2016 www.transparency.org/news/feature/asia_pacific_fighting_corruption_is_side_lined (all accessed November 7, 2017).

United Nations General Assembly. http://repository.un.org/bitstream/handle/11176/291712/A_RES_65_309-EN.pdf?sequence=3&isAllowed=y (accessed November 22, 2017).

World Happiness Report: http://worldhappiness.report/ (accessed November 22, 2017).

World Values Survey. www.worldvaluessurvey.org/wvs.jsp (accessed November 17, 2017).

2 Subjective wellbeing (I)

Satisfaction with life, life domains and living in Singapore

Subjective wellbeing (SWB) is a multifaceted concept that comprises people's life satisfaction, their evaluation of their life domains such as work, health and relationships, and how they think and feel about these aspects of their lives (Diener and Biswas-Diener 2008). Research in this area focuses on measuring an individual's cognitive and affective perceptions of and reactions to her or his whole life as well as to specific domains of life (Diener 1984; Myers and Diener 1995; Diener 2006). While affective measures focus on the presence of positive emotions or the absence of negative emotions, other measures emphasize life satisfaction, that is, a more cognitive sense of satisfaction with life (Diener and Suh 1997). These conceptualizations of the cognitive and affective aspects of wellbeing are aligned with the "hedonism of happiness" approach. Higher levels of life satisfaction and positive emotions are supposed to lead to greater levels of subjective wellbeing. A different but complementary approach is that of "the eudaimonism of happiness," which focuses on the intrinsic meaning of life and the fulfillment of life goals and skills (Seligman 2012), engagement and other aspects of psychological flourishing (Diener and Biswas-Diener 2008), and positive functioning (Sen 1993).

In our QOL Surveys, we have incorporated both approaches in our theoretical conceptualization, measurement and analysis. In this chapter, we discuss the more cognitive aspects of subjective wellbeing such as satisfaction with life, satisfaction with specific life domains and satisfaction with the overall quality of life, and satisfaction with various aspects of life in Singapore and satisfaction with the overall quality of life in Singapore. The more affective aspects of subjective wellbeing and psychological flourishing will be covered in Chapter 3.

Life satisfaction

Life satisfaction is an information-based evaluation and thus reflects the perceived distance between what is experienced and what is expected as a better life or envisioned as an ideal life. Cognitive wellbeing (or life satisfaction) is derived from a conscious judgment based on some standard. Affective wellbeing refers to feelings or emotional states that reflect spontaneous reactions to events in the individual's immediate experience.

Various types of economic, social and other indicators have been used in measuring life satisfaction. These indicators could be fairly objective, such as quantitative statistics with regard to per capita income, mortality rates, years of schooling and others (see Diener and Suh (1997) for a comprehensive review). Or they could be more subjective in nature and involve mainly perceptual measures in assessing the quality of life as experienced by a society's individuals. Some of these measures could be related to population density (Cramer et al. 2004), public safety (Inoguchi and Fujii 2009) and the quality of the area in which people live (Veenhoven 2012). Hellevik's (2003) study on happiness in the Norwegian population used five qualitative indicators to measure how a person perceives his or her economic or material situation: "satisfaction with income, satisfaction with possessions, feeling that the personal economy has been improving recently, expectations of future improvements, and finally, perceived relative economic situation compared to the population average" (p. 253).

Gudmundsdottir (2013) has analyzed how economic factors such as income might have a positive impact on life satisfaction but not on happiness. This is because people adapt to their level of wealth, resulting in wealthy people being only slightly happier than poorer people because the former inevitably end up wanting more and more. This could explain why there are poorer people who seemed contented with their lot in life (Olson and Schober 1993). Borooah (2006) has also suggested that comparison with others is an important factor in determining happiness and satisfaction, especially in terms of money. Hence, income would impact an individual's life satisfaction only if his or her income level was comparatively better than others. This positive correlation between income and wellbeing was prevalent only in poorer or less developed countries. The reason was that in richer countries, especially democracies, people have had most of their needs met by public goods provided by the government (Orviska et al. 2014). The relationship between income and cognitive measures of subjective wellbeing will be explored further in Chapter 4.

Diener and Tov (2012) suggested that research on wellbeing could incorporate more noneconomic indicators as there was a weak correlation between certain economic indicators (e.g., per capita income) and life satisfaction. Other indicators (e.g., relationships, feelings of belonging and long-term goals) could have an impact on satisfaction with life. Similarly, Glatzer (2012) proposed that smaller developed countries have an edge in terms of ensuring satisfaction for their citizens because of factors such as identity and sense of belonging.

Domain satisfaction

One common approach in measuring life satisfaction is to divide one's life into separate but different domains such as family, work, studies, health, and so on. This is known as "domain satisfaction," which depicts an enduring appreciation of certain aspects of life (Veenhoven 2012). Satisfaction with each of these domains can be assessed individually, and sometimes these assessments are collated to indicate an overall feeling of wellbeing (Kau and Wang 1995). Easterlin (2006) documented that income, family relations, job and health were the four key determinants of overall life satisfaction. Kapteyn et al. (2010) showed in their study of Dutch and American respondents that satisfaction with life was positively associated with satisfaction within each of these four domains, with the highest weight given to family and social relations, followed by job, health and income. Rath and Harter (2010) also concurred with this, stating that wellbeing essentially comprised of five elements: career wellbeing, social wellbeing, financial wellbeing, physical wellbeing and community wellbeing (Kruger 2010).

Studies have found that satisfaction with interpersonal relationships are important for wellbeing, such as family life and marriage (Campbell 1976) and friendships (Demir and Ozdemir 2010). This could be because interpersonal relationships meet an individual's psychological needs and make one feel important to others (Demir and Ozdemir 2010). The domain of health (both physical and mental aspects) also has an influence on people's happiness and life satisfaction (Borooah 2006).

For the 2016 QOL Survey, we have incorporated various measures on life satisfaction. Similar to the 2011 QOL Survey and the 2001 Survey, respondents were asked to indicate their satisfaction with various life domains and their satisfaction with overall quality of life. Fifteen life domains were covered in the 2016 QOL Survey. Respondents also gave their opinions on how satisfied they were with 25 aspects of living in Singapore and their satisfaction with overall quality of life in Singapore. For the 2016 QOL Survey, for the first time, we used the five-item Satisfaction with Life Scale (SWLS) developed by Diener et al. (1985). In this chapter, we report the satisfaction ratings for 2016, with comparisons to the 1996, 2001 and 2011 datasets when applicable.

Satisfaction with life domains and satisfaction with overall quality of life

Respondents in the survey were asked to rate their satisfaction with their life domains using a scale as follows: 1 for "very dissatisfied," 2 for "dissatisfied," 3 for "somewhat dissatisfied," 4 for "somewhat satisfied," 5 for "satisfied" and 6 for "very satisfied." Higher means thus indicated a greater degree of satisfaction. The 15 life domains were housing, friendships, marriage/romantic relationship, relationship with parents, relationship with children, relationship with brothers/sisters, relationship with neighbors, standard of living, household income, health, education attained, job (for those who are working full-time), studies (for those who are studying), leisure activities/entertainment and spiritual life. Table 2.1 shows the distribution of responses for the 15 life domains and satisfaction with overall quality of life. Singaporeans were most satisfied with the relationships with their children, parents and siblings, with their spiritual lives and with their friendships. They were most dissatisfied with their household

Table 2.1 Frequency distribution of responses to satisfaction with life domains and satisfaction with overall quality of life (2016)

Life domains	1[1] (%)	2 (%)	3 (%)	4 (%)	5 (%)	6 (%)	Mean (rank)
Household income	1.9	7.1	11.8	32.3	43.1	3.8	4.19 (15)
Friendships	0.1	2.0	4.1	22.0	61.5	10.4	4.74 (5)
Marriage/romantic relationship	1.6	4.4	5.8	15.7	53.3	19.2	4.72 (6)
Job (if you are working)	1.1	3.5	7.4	26.5	50.8	10.7	4.54 (12)
Studies (if studying part-/full-time)	1.8	3.9	8.4	28.8	48.6	8.4	4.44 (14)
Relationship with your parents	0.2	1.3	3.0	12.3	57.8	25.4	5.02 (2)
Relationship with your children	0.3	0.5	1.6	9.4	58.6	29.6	5.14 (1)
Relationship with brothers/sisters	0.5	1.3	3.1	15.7	58.5	20.9	4.93 (3)
Leisure activities/ entertainment	0.1	2.1	3.6	25.7	58.9	9.5	4.70 (8)
Relationship with neighbors	0.3	1.3	5.4	29.0	55.5	8.6	4.64 (9)
Standard of living	1.1	3.2	7.1	25.3	55.6	7.9	4.55 (11)
Health	0.9	2.9	6.3	21.5	60.1	8.3	4.62 (10)
Education attained	0.8	5.1	9.4	25.0	52.6	7.1	4.45 (13)
Housing	0.7	1.9	5.3	19.5	62.3	10.4	4.72 (6)
Spiritual life	0.5	1.2	2.9	21.2	61.2	13.0	4.80 (4)
Satisfaction with overall quality of life	0.1	1.3	4.0	24.0	62.3	8.4	4.72

1 Measured on a 6-point scale: 1 = Very dissatisfied, 2 = Dissatisfied, 3 = Somewhat dissatisfied, 4 = Somewhat satisfied, 5 = Satisfied, 6 = Very satisfied.

incomes, studies (if studying part-/full-time), education attained, jobs (if they were working) and their standard of living.

Table 2.2 shows the mean ratings of satisfaction with life domains for the years 2016, 2011, 2001 and 1996. Some domains are not common across the four years, and these are indicated accordingly in the table. As shown in Table 2.2, consistently over 20 years and across the four surveys conducted in 1996, 2001, 2011 and 2016, Singaporeans were most satisfied with their relationship with their children. The relationship with one's parents also yielded a high level of satisfaction, as evidenced by its high means and ranks (2nd or 3rd) for the four surveys. Similarly, satisfaction with the relationship with one's siblings was also ranked relatively highly (3rd or 4th). Satisfaction with one's marriage/romantic relationship was second highest in satisfaction for 1996 but slipped to the 4th berth for both 2001 and 2011. In 2016, there was a further drop in satisfaction

Table 2.2 Mean ratings of satisfaction with life domains and satisfaction with overall quality of life (2016, 2011, 2001 and 1996)

Life domains	2016 Mean[1] (15 domains)	2011 Mean[1] (15 domains)	2001 Mean[1] (12 domains)	1996 Mean[1] (12 domains)
Relationship with your children	5.14 (1)	5.32 (1)	5.10 (1)	5.25 (1)
Relationship with your parents	5.02 (2)	5.17 (2)	5.06 (2)	5.05 (3)
Relationship with brothers/sisters	4.93 (3)	5.09 (3)	4.97 (3)	4.92 (4)
Marriage/ romantic relationship	4.72 (6)	4.88 (4)	4.96 (4)	5.08 (2)
Job (if you are working)	4.54 (12)	4.65 (11)	4.81 (5)	4.55 (7)
Health	4.62 (10)	4.72 (9)	4.79 (6)	4.75 (6)
Study (if studying full/part time)	4.44 (14)	4.75 (6)	4.78 (7)	4.49 (9)
Friends	4.74 (5)	4.84 (5)	4.77 (8)	4.77 (5)
Leisure activities/ entertainment	4.70 (8)	4.74 (7)	4.69 (9)	4.44 (11)
Your physical appearance	Not measured	Not measured	4.68 (10)	4.47 (10)
Material comfort	Not measured	Not measured	4.64 (11)	4.53 (8)
Money	Not measured	Not measured	4.57 (12)	4.25 (12)
Household income	4.19 (15)	4.34 (15)	Not measured	Not measured
Relationship with neighbors	4.64 (9)	4.61 (12)	Not measured	Not measured
Standard of living	4.55 (11)	4.50 (13)	Not measured	Not measured
Education attained	4.45 (13)	4.45 (14)	Not measured	Not measured
Housing	4.72 (6)	4.69 (10)	Not measured	Not measured
Spiritual life	4.80 (4)	4.74 (7)	Not measured	Not measured
Satisfaction with overall quality of life	4.72	4.83	4.81	4.77

1 Measured on a 6-point scale: 1 = Very Dissatisfied, 2 = Dissatisfied, 3 = Somewhat Dissatisfied, 4 = Somewhat satisfied, 5= Satisfied, 6= Very Satisfied.

Numbers in parentheses indicate ranking based on highest to lowest mean ratings.

(6th rank). The 4th spot was taken by satisfaction with one's spiritual life, which occupied the 7th spot in 2011.

Satisfaction with friends and the leisure activities/entertainment domain hovered around the same rankings (5th and 7th positions in 2011, and 5th and 8th positions in 2016 respectively). However, satisfaction with the health domain fell to the 9th position from its 6th position in 1996 and 2001. In 2016, this domain was ranked 10th. Satisfaction with one's job increased over the years from the 7th spot in 1996 to the 5th spot in 2001 but declined drastically to the 11th spot in 2011. It slipped one more rank (12th) in 2016. Generally over the last five years or so, satisfaction with one's job has not been highly ranked. Satisfaction with one's studies also did not fare well over the years. In 2016, this domain was ranked 14th, a drop from the 6th rank in 2011.

Generally, through the years, Singaporeans were most satisfied with their familial relationships, although the marriage/romantic relationships domain took a beating in 2016. Consistently, household income and education attained were at the bottom for both 2011 and 2016. From 2011 to 2016, the means fell across the board for 10 out of 15 domains. Slight improvements were noted for relationship with one's neighbors, the standard of living, housing and spiritual life. The overall satisfaction with life rating improved from 4.77 in 1996 to 4.81 in 2001 and then to 4.83 in 2011. However, the 2016 mean (4.72) showed a decline from 2011.

Satisfaction with aspects of living in Singapore and satisfaction with overall quality of life in Singapore

Respondents in the survey were asked to rate their satisfaction with living in Singapore using a scale as follows: 1 for "very dissatisfied," 2 for "dissatisfied," 3 for "somewhat dissatisfied," 4 for "somewhat satisfied," 5 for "satisfied" and 6 for "very satisfied." Twenty-five aspects of living in Singapore were examined: the public services available, the convenience of public transport, the amount of freedom, the quality of education, the quality of law enforcement, the way the government runs the country, the cost of living, the number of rules and regulations to be followed, the level of safety and security, the variety of leisure and recreational facilities, the protection of consumers, the affordability of properties, the affordability of cars, the availability of career opportunities, the quality of healthcare, the availability of healthcare, the affordability of healthcare, the range of products and services available, the quality of customer services, the social welfare system, the democratic system, the condition of the environment, the ratio of locals to foreigners, the state of culture and the arts and Singaporean identity. The last three aspects were newly introduced in the 2016 QOL Survey. Table 2.3 shows the distribution of responses for the 25 aspects of living in Singapore and satisfaction with overall quality of life in Singapore. Singaporeans were most satisfied with the following five aspects of living in Singapore: the level of safety and security, the public services available, the quality of law enforcement, the quality of education and the convenience of

Table 2.3 Frequency distribution of responses to satisfaction with aspects of living in Singapore and satisfaction with overall quality of life in Singapore (2016)

Aspects of living in Singapore	1[1] (%)	2 (%)	3 (%)	4 (%)	5 (%)	6 (%)	Mean (rank)
1. Public services available	0.3	1.1	2.7	14.3	66.8	14.8	4.91 (2)
2. Convenience of public transport	0.8	1.4	4.4	15.8	63.3	14.3	4.82 (5)
3. Amount of freedom you have	0.7	2.3	5.9	18.7	61.3	11.2	4.71 (6)
4. Quality of education.	0.6	1.5	4.5	15.0	62.5	15.9	4.85 (4)
5. Quality of law enforcement	0.5	1.1	3.9	15.4	63.5	15.5	4.87 (3)
6. Way the government runs the country	0.9	2.5	6.5	23.6	55.2	11.4	4.64 (11)
7. Cost of living	5.9	17.0	25.1	31.7	18.0	2.3	3.46 (23)
8. Number of rules and regulations to be followed	1.8	7.1	12.1	32.3	42.2	4.5	4.20 (19)
9. Level of safety and security in Singapore/ public security	0.2	0.6	1.1	13.9	63.9	20.3	5.02 (1)
10. Variety of leisure and recreational facilities	0.6	1.9	6.2	25.5	57.9	7.9	4.62 (12)
11. Protection of consumers	0.5	2.9	7.2	29.3	53.6	6.7	4.53 (14)
12. Affordability of properties	8.3	20.6	25.0	26.0	18.2	1.9	3.31 (24)
13. Affordability of cars	17.2	29.1	24.2	20.0	8.5	0.9	2.76 (25)
14. Availability of career opportunities	3.1	8.4	17.5	37.3	31.3	2.4	3.92 (20)
15. Quality of healthcare	1.0	1.8	5.8	24.4	57.2	9.9	4.65 (10)
16. Availability of healthcare	0.5	1.9	4.5	24.3	58.1	10.6	4.69 (8)
17. Affordability of healthcare	4.1	11.2	16.8	31.4	31.6	4.9	3.90 (21)
18. Range of products and services available	0.5	1.4	4.7	29.3	58.5	5.7	4.61 (13)
19. Quality of customer services	0.7	3.6	8.7	34.7	48.6	3.6	4.38 (18)
20. Social welfare system	1.1	2.9	9.5	30.3	51.8	4.3	4.42 (16)
21. Democratic system	2.1	3.2	8.0	31.6	50.2	5.0	4.40 (17)
22. Condition of the environment	0.5	1.7	3.2	24.5	61.8	8.3	4.70 (7)
23. Ratio of locals to foreigners	7.7	11.4	21.5	32.7	25.1	1.6	3.61 (22)
24. State of culture and the arts	0.6	2.6	7.9	33.6	51.5	3.9	4.44 (15)
25. Singaporean identity	1.3	2.3	5.4	22.2	57.6	11.2	4.66 (9)
26. Satisfaction with overall quality of life in Singapore	0.3	1.3	4.3	28.9	57.4	7.9	4.66

1 Measured on a 6-point scale: 1 = Very dissatisfied, 2 = Dissatisfied, 3 = Somewhat dissatisfied, 4 = Somewhat satisfied, 5 = Satisfied, 6 = Very satisfied.

public transport. The bottom five aspects are the affordability of cars, the affordability of properties, the cost of living, the ratio of locals to foreigners and the affordability of healthcare.

Table 2.4 shows the mean ratings of satisfaction with living in Singapore for 2016 compared to 2011, 2001 and 1996. In 2016, Singaporeans were the most satisfied with the level of safety and security, the public services available, the quality of law enforcement, the quality of education and the convenience of public transport. As shown in Table 2.4, across the years, respondents were consistently very satisfied with the level of safety and security in Singapore. Two other aspects, the quality of education and the quality of law enforcement, were among the top four in 2011 and 2016. In 1996, the second-ranked aspect was the public services available, which dropped to the 3rd spot in 2001 and then to the 5th spot in 2011. However, this aspect rebounded in 2016 and took the 2nd spot.

Table 2.4 Mean ratings of satisfaction with aspects of living in Singapore and satisfaction with overall quality of life in Singapore (2016, 2011, 2001 and 1996)

Aspects of living in Singapore	2016 mean[1] (25 aspects)	2011 mean[1] (22 aspects)	2001 mean[1] (19 aspects)	1996 mean[1] (16 aspects)
1. Public services available	4.91 (2)	4.61 (5)	4.55 (3)	4.90 (2)
2. Convenience of public transport	4.82 (5)	4.55 (7)	4.53 (5)	4.70 (4)
3. Amount of freedom you have	4.71 (6)	4.57 (6)	4.40 (9)	4.50 (8)
4. Quality of education	4.85 (4)	4.76 (3)	4.50 (6)	4.60 (7)
5. Quality of law enforcement	4.87 (3)	4.90 (2)	4.57 (2)	4.80 (3)
6. Way the government runs the country	4.64 (11)	4.74 (4)	4.54 (4)	4.70 (4)
7. Cost of living	3.46 (23)	3.59 (20)	4.01 (17)	3.70 (14)
8. Number of rules and regulations	4.20 (19)	4.27 (14)	4.18 (15)	4.00 (12)
9. Level of safety and security in Singapore	5.02 (1)	4.93 (1)	4.64 (1)	4.97 (1)
10. Variety of leisure and recreational facilities	4.62 (12)	4.42 (12)	4.40 (9)	4.50 (8)

(*Continued*)

Table 2.4 (Continued)

Aspects of living in Singapore	2016 mean[1] (25 aspects)	2011 mean[1] (22 aspects)	2001 mean[1] (19 aspects)	1996 mean[1] (16 aspects)
11. Protection of consumers	4.53 (14)	4.23 (15)	4.34 (12)	4.40 (10)
12. Affordability of properties	3.31 (24)	3.11 (21)	3.96 (18)	3.252 (15)
13. Affordability of cars	2.76 (25)	2.89 (22)	3.69 (19)	3.252 (15)
14. Availability of career opportunities	3.92 (20)	3.88 (18)	4.12 (16)	4.22 (11)
15. Quality of healthcare	4.65 (10)	4.47 (10)	4.43 (8)	4.68 (6)
16. Availability of healthcare	4.69 (8)	4.53 (9)	4.44 (7)	Not measured
17. Affordability of healthcare	3.90 (21)	3.69 (19)	4.22 (14)	3.97 (13)
18. Range of products and services available	4.61 (13)	4.43 (11)	4.35 (11)	Not measured
19. Quality of customer services	4.38 (18)	4.07 (17)	4.31 (13)	Not measured
20. Social welfare system	4.42 (16)	4.16 (16)	Not measured	Not measured
21. Democratic system	4.40 (17)	4.37 (13)	Not measured	Not measured
22. Condition of the environment	4.70 (7)	4.54 (8)	Not measured	Not measured
23. The ratio of locals to foreigners	3.61 (22)	Not measured	Not measured	Not measured
24. The state of culture and the arts	4.44 (15)	Not measured	Not measured	Not measured
25. The Singaporean identity	4.66 (9)	Not measured	Not measured	Not measured
26. Satisfaction with overall quality of life in Singapore	4.66	4.41	4.50	4.67

1 Measured on a 6-point scale: 1 = Very dissatisfied, 2 = Dissatisfied, 3 = Somewhat dissatisfied, 4 = Somewhat satisfied, 5 = Satisfied, 6 = Very satisfied.
2 Items combined in 1996. Numbers in parentheses show rankings based on highest to lowest mean ratings.

In 2016, Singaporeans were most dissatisfied with the affordability of cars, the affordability of properties, the cost of living, the ratio of locals to foreigners and the affordability of healthcare. The first three of these issues were highlighted in 1996, 2001 and 2011. The affordability of healthcare was also a concern in 1996 and 2011. Thus, it seemed that for dissatisfaction with living in Singapore, these four aspects remained similar for the 20-year period considered. In 1996 and 2001, Singaporeans were disgruntled about the number of rules and regulations, but this did not surface in 2011 and 2016. The availability of career opportunities was more of a concern in 2001 and 2011 but not in 2016.

Improvements in satisfaction ratings were observed for the top five aspects of living in Singapore, except for the quality of law enforcement. From 2011 to 2016, satisfaction also increased for many aspects such as the amount of freedom (ranked 6th), the condition of the environment (ranked 7th), the availability of healthcare (ranked 8th), the quality of healthcare (ranked 10th), the variety of leisure and recreational facilities (ranked 12th), the range of products and services available (ranked 13th), the protection of consumers (ranked 14th), the social welfare system (ranked 16th) and the democratic system (ranked 17th). Although the satisfaction ratings increased for the affordability of properties (ranked 24th) and the affordability of healthcare (ranked 21st), Singaporeans were still largely dissatisfied with these two aspects of living in Singapore, as seen in their overall ranks. On the whole, 17 out of 22 common domains surveyed in 2011 and 2016 showed improvements in satisfaction ratings.

The five common aspects that showed decreases in satisfaction ratings were the quality of law enforcement (ranked 3rd), the way the government runs the country (ranked 11th), the number of rules and regulations (ranked 19th), the cost of living (ranked 23rd) and the affordability of cars (ranked 25th). The means for the overall satisfaction with living in Singapore dipped from 4.67 in 1996 to 4.5 in 2001 and then to 4.41 to 2011. However, in 2016, the mean improved to 4.66. In summary, it appeared that Singaporeans were still fairly less satisfied with living in Singapore (although the 2016 mean of 4.66 was higher than the 2011 mean of 4.41) than about life in general (although the 2016 mean of 4.72 was the lowest in 20 years).

Satisfaction with life scale

As this is the first time we are using the Satisfaction with Life Scale for our QOL Survey, we ran a factor analysis on the scale items. All the scale items loaded on one factor with 66.23 percent of the variance explained. The Cronbach alpha of 0.860 for the scale indicated a good level of reliability. For the overall sample, Singaporeans were generally satisfied with their lives (mean of 4.51) and felt they had the important things in life (mean of 4.42). (See Table 2.5.)

Table 2.5 Frequency distribution of responses to satisfaction with life (2016)

Domains	1[1] (%)	2 (%)	3 (%)	4 (%)	5 (%)	6 (%)	Mean (rank)
1. In most ways my life is close to my ideal.	0.9	6.0	9.4	35.2	45.2	3.3	4.28 (4)
2. The conditions of my life are excellent.	0.8	5.4	10.2	33.5	45.9	4.2	4.31 (3)
3. I am satisfied with my life.	0.7	4.0	7.4	25.9	55.5	6.5	4.51 (1)
4. So far I have gotten the important things I want in life.	0.9	6.0	8.3	27.3	50.1	7.4	4.42 (2)
5. If I could live my life over, I would change almost nothing.	3.5	13.7	18.6	21.2	37.5	5.5	3.92 (5)

1 Measured on a 6-point scale: 1 = Strongly disagree, 2 = Disagree 3 = Slightly disagree, 4 = Slightly agree, 5 = Agree, 6 = Strongly agree.

The impact of demographic variables on life satisfaction

Researchers have found that demographic variables such as age, education, income, race, employment and marital status were correlated at varying degrees to perceptions of life satisfaction (e.g., Oswald 1997; Blanchflower and Oswald 2000). Some of these correlations were weak, with less than 10 percent of the variance explained (Andrews and Withey 1974; Davis et al. 1982; Veenhoven 1984; Michalos 1985). For the QOL Surveys in Singapore, we usually present and discuss the sources of individual differences due to demographics as they provide additional insights into what matters for various segments of Singaporeans.

Table 2.6 shows the sources of individual differences for the top five most satisfied life domains for Singaporeans in 2016. Females were generally more satisfied than males, although the means were similar for friendship. The differences were not statistically significant for the various life domains except for relationship with children and spiritual life. For marital status, we included the 70 respondents who self-identified as "single" and answered the question on the relationship with one's children. Married respondents were significantly more satisfied with their relationships with their children and parents and with their spiritual life. The effect of age was significant for respondents in their 40s, 30s and 60s who were more satisfied with the relationship with their children. Respondents in their 40s to 60s were also significantly more satisfied with their relationship with their parents. As one got older, satisfaction with spiritual life rose. The youngest (15–19 years) and the oldest (70 years and above) reported the highest satisfaction with friendship.

Levels of satisfaction with the relationships with one's children and parents were significantly higher for those who had medium levels of education. Those with low-medium household incomes were significantly more satisfied with the relationships with their children and parents.

Table 2.7 shows the sources of individual differences for the top five most dissatisfied life domains for 2016. Females were more dissatisfied with regard to

Table 2.6 Sources of individual differences for top five most satisfied life domains (2016)

Demographics	1st domain: relationship with children	2nd domain: relationship with parents	3rd domain: relationship with brothers/sisters	4th domain: spiritual life	5th domain: friends
Gender					
• Male	5.09	5.01	4.92	4.77	4.74
• Female	5.19	5.03	4.95	4.83	4.74
• *F*-stats	**4.295**	0.113	0.364	**2.370**	0.012
• *p*<	**.038**	N.S.	N.S.	**0.124**	N.S.
Marital status					
• Single	4.67	4.92	4.90	4.67	4.74
• Married	5.20	5.06	4.95	4.86	4.76
• *F*-stats	37.988	7.282	0.873	17.363	0.127
• *p*<	.000	.007	N.S.	.000	N.S.
Age					
• 15–19	4.93	4.97	5.02	4.69	4.92
• 20–29	5.01	4.94	4.90	4.67	4.77
• 30–39	5.21	4.90	4.90	4.67	4.65
• 40–49	5.24	5.11	4.98	4.79	4.78
• 50–59	5.06	5.13	4.89	4.92	4.72
• 60–69	5.14	5.20	4.95	4.88	4.66
• 70 and above	5.12	4.86	4.96	5.04	4.81
• *F*-stats	**2.073**	**3.555**	0.620	**5.475**	**2.257**
• *p*<	**.054**	**.002**	N.S.	**.000**	**.036**
Education					
• Low	5.02	5.02	4.83	4.84	4.63
• Medium	5.19	5.07	4.97	4.80	4.76
• High	5.13	4.94	4.90	4.78	4.75
• *F*-stats	**4.447**	**2.995**	2.780	0.370	2.776
• *p*<	**.012**	**.050**	N.S	N.S.	N.S
Household income					
• Low	5.06	4.98	4.87	4.74	4.64
• Low-medium	5.28	5.08	4.94	4.75	4.69
• Medium-high	5.06	4.96	4.87	4.80	4.70
• High	5.22	4.74	4.85	4.63	4.79
• *F*-stats	**3.880**	**2.954**	0.524	0.627	0.692
• *p*<	**.009**	**.032**	N.S.	N.S.	N.S.

N.S. = Not significant.

Bold figures indicate significance.

Table 2.7 Sources of individual differences for top five most dissatisfied life domains (2016)

Demographics	1st domain: household income	2nd domain: study	3rd domain: education attained	4th domain: job	5th domain: standard of living
Gender					
• Male	4.24	4.41	4.47	4.50	4.52
• Female	4.15	4.47	4.43	4.59	4.57
• *F*-stats	2.649	0.438	0.628	1.892	1.396
• *p*<	N.S.	N.S.	N.S.	N.S.	N.S.
Marital status					
• Single	4.13	4.49	4.60	4.34	4.61
• Married	4.26	4.42	4.43	4.63	4.54
• *F*-stats	**4.614**	0.551	**9.547**	**15.518**	1.592
• *p*<	**.032**	N.S.	**.002**	**.000**	N.S.
Age					
• 15–19	4.44	4.50	4.72	4.73	4.90
• 20–29	4.08	4.45	4.68	4.36	4.59
• 30–39	4.05	4.32	4.60	4.44	4.48
• 40–49	4.20	4.51	4.47	4.57	4.51
• 50–59	4.26	4.46	4.35	4.64	4.49
• 60–69	4.24	4.41	4.09	4.80	4.44
• 70 and above	4.24	4.17	4.16	4.86	4.65
• *F*-stats	**2.569**	0.475	**11.622**	**3.118**	**3.895**
• *p*<	**.018**	N.S.	**.000**	**.005**	**.001**
Education					
• Low	4.07	4.00	3.64	4.63	4.33
• Medium	4.16	4.34	4.42	4.56	4.53
• High	4.32	4.79	4.94	4.50	4.70
• *F*-stats	**5.031**	**13.397**	**150.000**	0.634	**11.794**
• *p*<	**.007**	**.000**	**.000**	N.S.	**.000**
Household income					
• Low	3.71	4.31	4.15	4.36	4.24
• Low-medium	4.10	4.41	4.53	4.48	4.58
• Medium-high	4.38	4.46	4.59	4.40	4.61
• High	4.70	4.50	4.77	4.58	5.00
• *F*-stats	**27.244**	0.456	**14.919**	0.803	**17.877**
• *p*<	**.000**	N.S.	**.000**	N.S.	**.000**

N.S. = Not significant.

Bold figures indicate significance.

household incomes and education attained, while males were more dissatisfied with studies, jobs and standard of living. However, the differences were not statistically significant. Singles were less dissatisfied with regard to studies and education attained but more dissatisfied about household incomes, jobs and standard of living. The age effect was varied. The teenagers (15–19 years) were least dissatisfied about their household incomes, education attained and standard of living. This result should be interpreted with caution as these teenagers were not likely to be working and had some way to go in their education. Respondents in their 60s and 70s were more dissatisfied with education attained and less dissatisfied with jobs. Education and income both had an impact on dissatisfaction ratings. Those with less education and income were significantly more dissatisfied about their household incomes, education attained, and standard of living. In addition, those who were less educated were dissatisfied with studies.

Conclusion

In terms of satisfaction with life domains, across the four surveys conducted in 1996, 2001, 2011 and 2016, Singaporeans were most satisfied with their familial relationships, although satisfaction with marriage/romantic relationships was lower in 2016. Consistently, Singaporeans were most dissatisfied with their household income and level of education in 2011 and 2016. In terms of satisfaction with overall quality of life, Singaporeans' rating on this item registered a gradual increase from 1996 to 2011, but it dipped slightly in 2016.

In 2016, the top five areas in which Singaporeans were the most satisfied with living in Singapore were related to the availability and quality of public services and the infrastructure: the level of safety and security, the public services available, the quality of law enforcement, the quality of education, and the convenience of public transport. Aspects relating to public services and the infrastructure were also consistently ranked among the top five by Singaporeans in the surveys of 1996, 2001 and 2011. In 2016, Singaporeans were the least satisfied with five areas, which were mostly related to affordable and comfortable living in Singapore: the affordability of cars, the affordability of properties, the cost of living, the ratio of locals to foreigners, and the affordability of healthcare. Consistently, the affordability issues were also the top main grouses of Singaporeans in the surveys of 1996, 2001 and 2011 (with the exception of the aspect relating to the ratio of locals to foreigners, which was not included in these surveys). Unlike their satisfaction with the overall quality of life, Singaporeans' satisfaction with the overall quality of life in Singapore registered an increase, thus reversing the declining trend since 2001.

We incorporated the Satisfaction with Life Scale for the first time in our 2016 QOL Survey, and our analysis confirmed its unidimensionality and good reliability. The scale showed Singaporeans to be generally satisfied with their lives (mean of 4.51), which corresponded well to what we have found for the satisfaction with overall quality of life (mean of 4.72) and for satisfaction with the overall quality of life in Singapore (mean of 4.66).

The influence of certain demographic variables on life satisfaction was investigated in the 2016 QOL Survey. Age and education were the main driving forces, accounting for four out of five top life domains that Singaporeans were satisfied with, followed by marital status (three out of five domains). Gender and household income were less influential (accounting for two out of five domains). Individual differences due to age and education were repeated for the top five domains that Singaporeans were dissatisfied with, followed by marital status and household income (accounting for three out of five domains), while gender had no impact.

As mentioned at the beginning of this chapter, researchers have highlighted the importance of incorporating more noneconomic indicators such as relationships when examining wellbeing and life satisfaction. Our four QOL surveys (1996, 2001, 2011 and 2016) have incorporated various relationship domains when examining Singaporeans' life satisfaction and found these to be important drivers of wellbeing.

References

Andrews, F.M., and Withey, S.B. (1974), 'Developing measures of perceived life quality: Results from several national surveys', *Social Indicators Research*, 1, 1–26.

Blanchflower, D.G., and Oswald, A.J. (2000), *Wellbeing over time in Britain and the USA*, Cambridge, MA, USA: National Bureau of Economic Research.

Borooah, V.K. (2006), 'What makes people happy? Some evidence from Northern Ireland', *Journal of Happiness Studies*, 7, 427–465.

Campbell, A. (1976), 'Subjective measures of wellbeing', *American Psychologist*, 31, 117–124.

Cramer, V., Torgersen, S., and Kringlen, E. (2004), 'Quality of life in a city: The effect of population density', *Social Indicators Research*, 69, 103–116.

Davis, E.E., Fine-Davis, M., and Meehan, G. (1982), 'Demographic determinants of perceived wellbeing in eight European countries', *Social Indicators Research*, 10, 341–335.

Demir, M., and Ozdemir, M. (2010), 'Friendship, need satisfaction and happiness', *Journal of Happiness Studies*, 11, 243–259.

Diener, E. (1984), 'Subjective wellbeing', *Psychological Bulletin*, 95(3), 542–575.

Diener, E. (2006), 'Guidelines for national indicators of subjective wellbeing and ill-being', *Journal of Happiness Studies*, 7(4), 397–404.

Diener, E., and Biswas-Diener, R. (2008), *Happiness: Unlocking the mysteries of psychological wealth*, New York, NY, USA: Blackwell.

Diener, E., Emmons, R.A., Larsen, R.J., and Griffin, S. (1985), 'The Satisfaction with Life Scale', *Journal of Personality Assessment*, 49, 71–75.

Diener, E., and Suh, M. (1997), 'Subjective wellbeing and age: An international analysis', *Annual Review of Gerontology and Geriatrics*, 17, 304–324.

Diener, E. and Tov, W. (2012), 'National accounts of wellbeing', in *Handbook of social indicators and quality of life research*, New York, NY, USA: Springer.

Easterlin, R.A. (2006), 'Life cycle happiness and its sources: Intersections of psychology, economics, and demography', *Journal of Economic Psychology*, 27(4), 463–482.

Glatzer, W. (2012), 'Cross-national comparisons of quality of life in developed nations, including the impact of globalization', *Handbook of social indicators and quality of life research*, edited by K. Land, A. Michalos and M. Sirgy, Dordrecht, Netherlands: Springer, 381–398.

Gudmundsdottir, D.G. (2013), 'The impact of economic crisis on happiness', *Social Indicators Research*, 110, 1083–1101.

Hellevik, O. (2003), 'Economy, values and happiness in Norway', *Journal of Happiness Studies*, 4, 243–283.

Inoguchi, T. and Fujii, S. (2009), 'The quality of life in Japan', *Social Indicators Research*, 92, 227–262.

Kapteyn, A., Smith, J.P., and van Soest, A. (2010), 'Life satisfaction', in *International differences in well-being*, edited by E. Diener, D. Kahneman and J. Helliwell, Oxford, UK: Oxford University Press, 70–104.

Kau, A.K., and Wang, S.H. (1995), 'Assessing quality of life in Singapore: An exploratory study', *Social Indicators Research*, 35, 71–91.

Kruger, P.S. (2010), 'Wellbeing: The five essential elements', *Applied Research in Quality of Life*, 6(3), 325–328.

Michalos, A.C. (1985), 'Multiple discrepancies theory (MDT)', *Social Indicators Research*, 16, 347–414.

Myers, D.G., and Diener, E. (1995), 'Who is happy?', *Psychological Science*, 6, 10–19.

Olson, G.L., and Schober, B.I. (1993), 'The satisfied poor', *Social Indicators Research*, 28, 173–193.

Orviska, M., Caplanova, A. and Hudson, J. (2014), 'The impact of democracy on well-being', *Social Indicators Research*, 115(1), 493–508.

Oswald, A.J. (1997), 'Happiness and economic performance', *Economic Journal*, 107(445), 1815–1831.

Rath, T., and Harter, J. (2010), *Wellbeing: The five essential elements*, New York, NY, USA: Gallup Press.

Seligman, M. (2012), *Flourish: A visionary new understanding of happiness and wellbeing*, Hillsboro, OR, USA: Altraria Book.

Sen, A. (1993), 'Capability and wellbeing', in *The quality of life*, edited by M. Nussenbaum and A. Sen, Oxford, UK: Clarendon Press, 30–53.

Veenhoven, R. (1984), *Conditions of happiness*, Dordrecht, Netherlands: D. Reidel.

Veenhoven, R. (2012), 'Happiness also known as "life satisfaction" and "subjective well-being"', in *Handbook of social indicators and quality of life research*, New York, NY, USA: Springer.

3 Subjective wellbeing (II)
Happiness, enjoyment, achievement and other aspects

In Chapter 2, we discussed the more cognitive aspects of subjective wellbeing such as satisfaction with life, satisfaction with specific life domains and satisfaction with the overall quality of life, and satisfaction with various aspects of living in Singapore and satisfaction with the overall quality of life in Singapore. In this chapter, we discuss in greater detail other aspects of subjective wellbeing such as happiness, enjoyment, achievement, control over important aspects of life, a sense of purpose in life and psychological flourishing. Individual differences among these wellbeing indicators are also examined. When possible, comparisons are made with previous surveys in 2006 and 2011. Together, Chapters 2 and 3 present a multifaceted perspective of the subjective wellbeing of Singaporeans.

We first examine Singaporeans' affective aspects of their subjective wellbeing in terms of happiness, enjoyment, achievement, control and purpose. Questions on Happiness, Enjoyment, and Achievement were previously included in the 2006 AsiaBarometer Survey and the 2011 QOL Survey as indicators of overall life quality. For the 2016 QOL Survey, we added questions on control and purpose. These questions from Tinkler and Hicks' (2011) scales measure locus of control and sense of purpose.

For the 2011 QOL Survey, we used the 12-item Psychological Flourishing Scale developed by Diener and Biswas-Diener (2008) to measure another affective aspect of subjective wellbeing. The same scale was used in the 2016 QOL Survey. The scale has been used to classify respondents at different levels of psychological flourishing, from "extremely high flourishing" to "extremely low flourishing."

Happiness, enjoyment, achievement, control and purpose

Affective measures complement cognitive measures by highlighting the positive emotions that contribute to a person's subjective wellbeing. For instance, when happiness is used as an indicator of subjective wellbeing, we usually consider the hedonic level of affect or the pleasantness of hedonic experiences such as feelings, emotions and moods (Veenhoven 2012). Individuals have a substantial capacity for enjoyment, which is also an important indicator of the quality of life (Veenhoven 2012). The eudaimonic approach to understanding subjective wellbeing suggests that meaning and purpose are important contributors to the significance of one's life (Ryan and Deci 2001; Seligman 2012).

In this section, we report the 2016 QOL Survey findings for the indicators of happiness, enjoyment, achievement, control and purpose, which will give us more insights into Singaporeans' state of subjective wellbeing. For an indication of how happy Singaporeans are, respondents were asked in the 2016 QOL Survey to respond to the question "All things considered, would you say that you are happy these days?" on a rating scale of "1 = very unhappy," "2 = not too happy," "3 = neither happy nor unhappy," "4 = quite happy," and "5 = very happy." To assess enjoyment, respondents were asked to respond to the question "How often do you feel you are really enjoying life these days?" on a rating scale of "1 = never," "2 = rarely," "3 = sometimes," and "4 = often." For an indication of achievement, respondents were asked to respond to the question "How much do you feel you are accomplishing what you want out of your life?" on a rating scale of "1 = none," "2 = very little," "3 = some," and "4 = a great deal." To assess control, respondents were asked to respond to the question "How much control do you feel you have over important aspects of your life?" on a scale of "1 = none," "2 = very little," "3 = some," and "4 = a great deal." To assess purpose, respondents were asked to respond to the question "All things considered, how much do you feel you have a sense of purpose in your life?" on a scale of "1 = none," "2 = very little," "3 = some," and "4 = a great deal." To give us a sense of how Singaporeans fared in these indicators over time, we also compared our findings with the results from the 2006 AsiaBarometer Survey (Tambyah et al. 2010) and the 2011 QOL survey (Tambyah and Tan 2013).

Happiness, enjoyment and achievement

As shown in Table 3.1a, in terms of happiness, compared to ten years (2006) and five years (2011) ago, Singaporeans have become increasingly less happy. Only 10 percent of Singaporeans reported that they were "very happy" (compared to 19 percent in 2011 and 27.5 percent in 2006). There was also a slight dip for those who reported that they were "quite happy" (54 percent in 2016 compared to 55.2 percent in 2011), although the percentage was higher than 2006 (51.1 percent). More Singaporeans reported that they were "neither happy nor unhappy" (25 percent in 2016 compared to 20.6 percent in 2011 and 15.4 percent in 2006), "not too happy" (8.7 percent in 2016 compared to 4.7 percent in 2011 and 5.2 percent in 2006) and "very unhappy" (2.3 percent in 2016 compared to 0.5 percent in 2011 and 0.9 percent in 2006). The Happiness Index was down from +72.5 percent in 2006 to +69 percent in 2011 and slipped further to +53.0 percent in 2016.

Correspondingly, as shown in Table 3.1b, the percentages of those who reported that they enjoyed life "often" dropped from 34.3 percent in 2006 to 31.7 percent in 2011 and to a low of 21.6 percent in 2016. The percentages of those who reported "rarely" enjoying life rose from 10 percent in 2006 to 11.3 percent in 2011 and then to 16.8 percent in 2016. Like the Happiness Index, the Enjoyment Index took a beating, slipping to a low of 61.8 percent compared to over 75 percent in 2011 and 2006.

Singaporeans also reported low feelings of achievement (Table 3.1c), with the percentages of those who reported that they had accomplished "a great

Table 3.1a Levels of happiness

	Very happy (a) (%)	Quite happy (b) (%)	Neither happy nor unhappy (%)	Not too happy (c) (%)	Very unhappy (d) (%)	Happiness index (a + b) – (c + d) (%)
Percentages for 2006 AsiaBarometer Survey	27.5	51.1	15.4	5.2	0.9	+72.5
Percentages for 2011 QOL Survey	19.0	55.2	20.6	4.7	0.5	+69.0
Percentages for 2016 QOL Survey	10.0	54.0	25.0	8.7	2.3	+53.0

Table 3.1b Levels of enjoyment

	Often (a) (%)	Sometimes (b) (%)	Rarely (c) (%)	Never (d) (%)	Enjoyment index (a + b) – (c + d) (%)
Percentages for 2006 AsiaBarometer Survey	34.3	54.2	10.0	1.5	+77.0
Percentages for 2011 QOL Survey	31.7	56.1	11.3	0.8	+75.7
Percentages for 2016 QOL Survey	21.6	59.3	16.8	2.3	+61.8

Table 3.1c Levels of achievement

	A great deal (a) (%)	Some (b) (%)	Very little (c) (%)	None (d) (%)	Achievement index (a + b) – (c + d) (%)
Percentages for 2006 AsiaBarometer Survey	16.9	59.1	20.7	3.2	+52.1
Percentages for 2011 QOL Survey	21.2	61.7	15.3	1.8	+65.8
Percentages for 2016 QOL Survey	12.6	66.4	19.0	2.0	+58.0

deal" decreasing from 21.2 percent in 2011 to 12.6 percent in 2016, although those who felt that they had "some" accomplishment continued to increase from 59.1 percent in 2006 to 61.7 percent in 2011 and to 66.4 percent in 2016. Nevertheless, the Accomplishment Index showed a negative change from +65.8 percent in 2011 to +58 percent in 2016.

Control and purpose

Two-thirds (66.2 percent) of Singaporeans felt that they have some control over important aspects of their life, giving rise to a Control Index of 65 percent (see Table 3.2a). This is the second highest index across the subjective wellbeing indicators. Close to two-thirds (65.4 percent) of Singaporeans reported that they have some Sense of Purpose in their lives, giving rise to a Sense of Purpose Index of 71.4 percent, the highest index across the subjective wellbeing indicators.

Overall, it appears that over the last ten years, Singaporeans were less happy and enjoyed life less. The Happiness and Enjoyment Indexes decreased from 2006 to 2011 and then again from 2011 to 2016. The Achievement Index rose from 2006 to 2011 but dropped in 2016. However, Singaporeans still felt they had some control over their lives and a sense of purpose as shown in the Control and Purpose Indexes. These two indexes were newly added in 2016, and we do not have data from 2006 and 2011 to comment on any movement.

Table 3.2a Levels of control

	A great deal (a) (%)	*Some* (b) (%)	*Very little* (c) (%)	*None* (d) (%)	*Control index* (a + b) − (c + d) (%)
Percentages for 2016 QOL Survey	16.3	66.2	16.0	1.5	+65.0

Table 3.2b Levels of sense of purpose

	A great deal (a) (%)	*Some* (b) (%)	*Very little* (c) (%)	*None* (d) (%)	*Sense of purpose index* (a + b) − (c + d) (%)
Percentages for 2016 QOL Survey	20.3	65.4	12.3	2.0	+71.4

The Sense of Purpose Index (highest among the five indexes) was correlated with the increase in the number of Singaporeans who felt that they had made some achievements (the only indicator, that is, the Achievement Index, to report an increase from 2006 to 2011). Hence, Singaporeans appeared to be achievement oriented with a sense of purpose.

Individual differences for subjective wellbeing indicators

How do certain demographic variables correlate with measures of happiness, enjoyment, achievement, control and purpose? Some researchers have posited a U-shaped relationship between age and subjective wellbeing, with younger and older people reporting high levels of happiness while middle-aged people were often overwhelmed with responsibilities and were too busy and tired to enjoy life (Oswald 1997; Blanchflower and Oswald 2000).

For social class, there is usually a small positive relationship between income and happiness; a similar effect is noted for other social class indicators such as education and occupational status. In Japan, those with at least a high school education were happier than those without by a factor of almost 1.5 (Inoguchi and Fujii 2009). The quality of the area in which people lived was another indicator of social class that influenced the happiness of individuals and communities. People in higher occupational classes, who lived in better and safer neighborhoods, described themselves as happier than those in the lower classes (Veenhoven 2012). The relationship between income and affective measures of subjective wellbeing will be explored further in Chapter 4.

Generally, for marital status, research studies have shown that married people rated themselves as happier than single or divorced people (Veroff et al. 1981; Diener et al. 2000). However, the happiness differential between married and never married individuals could be narrowing, with never married individuals experiencing increasing happiness, and the married experiencing decreasing happiness (Lee et al. 1991). This could be because of fewer and later marriages and rising divorce rates.

In Singapore, our 2016 QOL Survey shows that age had a significant relationship with Achievement (see second row of Table 3.3), where a sense of achievement increased as age increased. Education was positively correlated with all five indicators: Happiness, Enjoyment, Achievement, Control and Sense of Purpose (see third row of Table 3.3). This held true for Household Income too (see fifth row of Table 3.3). The means for these subjective wellbeing indicators increased as education and income increased. Gender did not matter for any of the five indicators (see fourth row of Table 3.3), while marital status was positively correlated with achievement, control and sense of purpose (see sixth row of Table 3.3). Married respondents were happier than single respondents, but this difference was not statistically significant.

Thus, it appeared that in Singapore, if you felt that you had accomplished more, had more control over important aspects of your life, and had more purpose in life, you were likely to be older and married and had more education and higher income, regardless of your gender.

Table 3.3 Individual differences in means for happiness, enjoyment, achievement, control and purpose (2016)

Demographics	Happiness	Enjoyment	Achievement	Control	Sense of purpose
Age					
• 15–24	3.60	3.06	2.83	2.97	3.03
• 25–34	3.59	3.02	2.82	2.92	2.99
• 35–44	3.60	2.96	2.92	2.99	3.06
• 45–54	3.58	2.98	2.89	2.96	3.07
• 55–64	3.66	3.05	2.96	3.00	3.07
• 65 and above	3.63	2.97	2.98	2.99	3.01
• F-stats	0.300	0.897	**2.611**	0.514	0.648
• p<	N.S.	N.S.	**.023**	N.S.	N.S.
Education					
• Low	3.55	2.78	2.77	2.86	2.85
• Medium	3.57	2.99	2.86	2.95	3.03
• High	3.71	3.14	3.05	3.08	3.15
• F-stats	**3.787**	**21.140**	**19.052**	**11.419**	**16.598**
• p<	**.023**	**.000**	**.000**	**.000**	**.000**
Gender					
• Male	3.58	2.99	2.88	2.97	3.03
• Female	3.64	3.01	2.91	2.97	3.05
• F-Stats	1.721	0.499	0.932	0.030	0.441
• p<	N.S.	N.S.	N.S.	N.S.	N.S.
Household income					
• Low	3.41	2.84	2.71	2.80	2.86
• Medium-low	3.58	3.08	2.93	3.03	3.11
• Medium-high	3.61	3.17	2.97	3.06	3.17
• High	3.70	3.22	3.22	3.25	3.30
• F-Stats	**3.720**	**11.946**	**16.946**	**14.855**	**16.582**
• p<	**.011**	**.000**	**.000**	**.000**	**.000**
Marital status					
• Single	3.58	3.01	2.79	2.92	2.98
• Married	3.64	3.01	2.95	3.01	3.08
• F-stats	1.357	.001	**20.226**	**7.052**	**8.046**
• p<	N.S	N.S.	**.000**	**.008**	**.005**

N.S. = Not significant.

Bold figures indicate significance.

Age and its relationship with the subjective wellbeing indicators varied over the years. In 2006, Happiness and Enjoyment did not vary significantly across age groups, but Singaporeans in the 40- to 49-year age group felt that they had not achieved a lot. In 2011, Happiness, Enjoyment and Achievement varied significantly across age groups, with young Singaporeans between the ages of 25 and 34 years being the least happy, enjoying life the least, and perceiving themselves as not having achieved a lot compared to other age groups (Tambyah and Tan 2013). In 2016, there were no statistically significant differences for Happiness and Achievement across age groups, although it can be noted that the 25- to 34-year age group had the second lowest mean for Happiness and the lowest mean for Achievement.

The significant correlations between education and household income with all five indicators showed some interesting differences with what were found in the 2006 and 2011 Surveys. Although education played no significant role in Singaporeans' happiness in 2006, it varied significantly with Singaporeans' enjoyment and achievement, where the tertiary educated Singaporeans indicated that they not only enjoyed life the most but also felt that they had accomplished a lot. However, in 2011, Happiness, Enjoyment and Achievement did not vary significantly across different educational levels. In 2006, Singaporeans with medium household incomes were the happiest and enjoyed life most, while those with high household incomes felt they had achieved a lot. In 2011, Singaporeans with high household incomes were the happiest, enjoyed life the most, and felt that they had achieved a lot, while those with low household incomes felt the least in terms of happiness, enjoyment and achievement.

The absence of a significant correlation between gender and the Happiness, Enjoyment and Achievement indicators in 2016 was consistent with what Tambyah and Tan (2013) found in the 2006 and 2011 surveys, where the mean scores for all three indicators did not vary in a statistically significant way for males and females. The absence of significant correlations between marital status and the Happiness, Enjoyment, and Achievement indicators in 2016 was not consistent with past surveys mentioned in Tambyah and Tan (2013). In 2006 and 2011, married Singaporeans were happier than single Singaporeans, although in both years, marital status did not matter for Singaporeans' Enjoyment. However, unlike 2016 and 2006, married Singaporeans felt that they had accomplished more than their single counterparts in 2011.

Psychological flourishing

Psychological flourishing is an important topic that has garnered considerable research interest (Hone et al. 2014). Psychological flourishing "goes beyond an individual's pursuit of her own happiness to include her contributions to society and the happiness of others" (Diener and Biswas-Diener 2008, p. 241). The original 12-item Psychological Flourishing Scale (see Table 3.4) developed by Diener and Biswas-Diener (2008) measures whether major aspects of psychological wealth are present in one's life and whether one's life has purpose and meaning. Since then, Diener et al. (2010) have revised this to an 8-item scale, omitting items 7, 8, 9 and 11 in Table 3.4. It was renamed the Flourishing Scale, and it had a one-factor structure with a Cronbach alpha of 0.87. The Flourishing Scale has been validated in various countries and contexts, for instance

Table 3.4 The 12-Item Psychological Flourishing Scale

Psychological Flourishing Scale (7-point scale, 1 = Strong disagreement to 7 = Strong agreement)

1. I lead a purposeful and meaningful life.
2. My social relationships are supportive and rewarding.
3. I am engaged and interested in my daily activities.
4. I actively contribute to the happiness and wellbeing of others.
5. I am competent and capable in the activities that are important to me.
6. I am a good person and live a good life.
7. My material life (income, housing, etc.) is sufficient for my needs.
8. I generally trust others and feel part of my community.
9. I am satisfied with my religious or spiritual life.
10. I am optimistic about the future.
11. I have no addictions, such as to alcohol, illicit drugs, or gambling.
12. People respect me.

Source: Diener and Biswas-Diener (2008).

Table 3.5 Interpretation of psychological flourishing scores

Score range	What it means
80–84	Extremely high flourishing
74–79	Very high flourishing
68–73	High flourishing
60–67	Flourishing
48–59	Slight lack of flourishing
32–47	Lack of flourishing
12–31	Extremely low flourishing

Source: Diener and Biswas-Diener (2008).

in Egypt (Salama-Younes 2017), France (Villieux et al. 2016), Japan (Sumi 2013), New Zealand (Hone et al. 2014) and Portugal (Silva and Caetano 2013).

For the 12-item Psychological Flourishing Scale, Diener and Biswas-Diener (2008) provided a possible score range to guide the interpretations of what the numbers mean in terms of psychological flourishing (see Table 3.5). However, for the 8-item Flourishing Scale, Diener et al. (2010) did not provide any specific interpretation of the scores, but only "norms for the scale in terms of percentiles" (p. 149) and noted that "a high score represents a person with many psychological resources and strengths" (p. 155).

Similar to the 2011 QOL Survey, we used the 12-item Psychological Flourishing Scale in the 2016 QOL Survey. A principal component factor analysis showed that this 12-item scale had a Cronbach alpha of 0.886, while the 8-item scale had a Cronbach alpha of 0. 891. Hence to facilitate comparisons with the 2011

Table 3.6 Singaporeans' psychological flourishing scores (2016 and 2011 QOL Surveys)

Regrossed score range	What it means	2016 number and percentage of Singaporeans (N = 1503)	2011 number and percentage of Singaporeans (N = 1496, 4 missing)
68–72	Extremely high flourishing	41 (2.7%)	29 (1.9%)
63–67	Very high flourishing	68 (4.5%)	98 (6.5%)
58–62	High flourishing	660 (43.9%)	598 (40%)
53–57	Flourishing	328 (21.8%)	564 (37.7%)
48–52	Slight lack of Flourishing	261 (17.4%)	200 (13.4%)
32–47	Lack of Flourishing	141 (9.4%)	7 (0.5%)
12–31	Extremely low flourishing	4 (0.3%)	0 (0%)

QOL Survey, we decided to use the 12-item scale along with Diener and Biswas-Diener's (2008) interpretation of the scores.

Similar to the 2011 QOL Survey, we standardized the design of questions. To avoid confusing the respondents, we formatted the Psychological Flourishing Scale to be a 6-point scale. Hence we need to regross the score range in order to use Diener and Biswas-Diener's (2008) interpretation. The regrossed range is shown in Table 3.6 with the distribution of Singaporeans' scores on psychological flourishing for 2016 compared with the 2011 QOL Survey.

Table 3.6 shows that, compared to 2011, in 2016 there was a slight increase in the percentage of Singaporeans who were in the Extremely High Flourishing range (2.7 percent versus 1.9 percent) and in the majority of Singaporeans who were in the High Flourishing range (43.9 percent versus 40 percent). However, there was a slight decrease in the percentage of Singaporeans who were in the Very High Flourishing range (from 6.5 percent in 2011 to 4.5 percent in 2016) and the Flourishing range (from 37.7 percent in 2011 to 21.8 percent in 2016). Overall, there was a decline in the overall psychological flourishing score in 2016, where only seven out of ten (72.9 percent) scored 53 and above, compared to eight out of ten (86.1 percent) in 2011.

Table 3.7 shows where the individual differences can occur for Singaporeans' psychological flourishing. There was a good distribution of High Flourishing Singaporeans across all age groups, although there were fewer Flourishing Singaporeans in the 15- to 24-year age group compared to the other age groups. There were also more Singaporeans in the 25- to 34-year age group who belonged to the Lack of Flourishing category. This pattern of response was similar to what Tambyah and Tan (2013) found in the 2011 QOL Survey. Age differences were less significant, with comparable numbers across the various age groups in both the High Flourishing and Flourishing categories.

Individual differences were evident for education. Singaporeans with medium and higher education formed the majority in the High Flourishing category,

Table 3.7 Individual differences for Singaporeans' psychological flourishing scores (2016)

Demographics	Extremely high flourishing	Very high flourishing	High flourishing	Flourishing	Slight lack of flourishing	Lack of flourishing	Extremely low flourishing
Total sample							
1503	41	68	660	328	261	141	4
(100%)	(2.7%)	(4.5%)	(43.9%)	(21.8%)	(17.4%)	(9.4%)	(0.3%)
Age groups (years)							
15 – 24	9	14	110	39	39	13	2
	(4.0%)	(6.2%)	(48.7%)	(17.3%)	(17.3%)	(5.8%)	(0.9%)
25 – 34	5	8	108	51	43	34	0
	(2.0%)	(3.2%)	(43.4%)	(20.5%)	(17.3%)	(13.7%)	(0%)
35 – 44	10	13	122	65	59	28	0
	(3.4%)	(4.4%)	(41.1%)	(21.9%)	(19.9%)	(9.4%)	(0%)
45 – 54	7	15	128	71	45	22	0
	(2.4%)	(5.2%)	(44.4%)	(24.7%)	(15.6%)	(7.6%)	(0%)
55 – 64	5	12	116	48	36	22	1
	(2.1%)	(5.0%)	(48.3%)	(20.0%)	(15.0%)	(9.2%)	(0.4%)
65 and above	5	6	76	54	39	22	1
	(2.5%)	(3.0%)	(37.4%)	(26.6%)	(19.2%)	(10.8%)	(0.5%)
Education							
Low	6	5	74	58	47	28	2
	(2.7%)	(2.3%)	(33.6%)	(26.4%)	(21.4%)	(12.7%)	(0.9%)
Medium	21	39	388	185	154	79	2
	(2.4%)	(4.5%)	(44.7%)	(21.3%)	(17.7%)	(9.1%)	(0.2%)
High	14	24	198	85	60	34	0
	(3.4%)	(5.8%)	(47.7%)	(20.5%)	(14.5%)	(8.2%)	(0%)

(Continued)

Table 3.7 (Continued)

Demographics	Extremely high flourishing	Very high flourishing	High flourishing	Flourishing	Slight lack of flourishing	Lack of flourishing	Extremely low flourishing
Gender							
Male	21	37	311	154	134	74	0
	(2.9%)	(5.1%)	(42.5%)	(21.1%)	(18.3%)	(10.1%)	(0%)
Female	20	31	349	174	127	67	4
	(2.6%)	(4.0%)	(45.2%)	(22.5%)	(16.5%)	(8.7%)	(0.5%)
Household income							
Low	6	15	124	73	72	63	1
	(1.7%)	(4.2%)	(35.0%)	(20.6%)	(20.3%)	(17.8%)	(0.3%)
Medium-low	12	21	124	82	67	30	1
	(3.6%)	(6.2%)	(36.8%)	(24.3%)	(19.9%)	(8.9%)	(0.3%)
Medium-high	4	8	74	44	28	15	0
	(2.3%)	(4.6%)	(42.8%)	(25.4%)	(16.2%)	(8.7%)	(0%)
High	6	7	28	21	10	4	1
	(7.8%)	(9.1%)	(36.4%)	(27.3%)	(13.0%)	(5.2%)	(1.3%)
Marital status							
Single	13	20	195	88	81	54	3
	(2.9%)	(4.4%)	(43.0%)	(19.4%)	(17.8%)	(11.9%)	(0.7%)
Married	23	42	420	208	155	73	1
	(2.5%)	(4.6%)	(45.6%)	(22.6%)	(16.8%)	(7.9%)	(0.1%)

while more Singaporeans in the Flourishing and Slight Lack of Flourishing categories had low education. In 2011, proportionately more respondents with medium and high levels of education were in the High Flourishing category.

Slightly more female Singaporeans were in the High Flourishing and Flourishing categories, while there were slightly more males in the Very High Flourishing, Slight Lack of Flourishing, and Lack of Flourishing categories. While females tended to be doing well, for males, there appeared to be a polarizing effect in terms of their psychological flourishing. This was in contrast to the 2011 QOL Survey where males and females were fairly equally distributed across the Very High Flourishing, High Flourishing, Flourishing, and Slight Lack of Flourishing categories.

Individual differences were also evident in psychological flourishing across levels of household incomes. More medium-high-income Singaporeans belonged to the High Flourishing category than the high-income or low- and medium-low-income Singaporeans, while the Flourishing category was fairly well distributed across all income groups. However, the Slight Lack of Flourishing and Lack of Flourishing categories were dominated by Singaporeans with low incomes. In 2011, more respondents in the High Flourishing belonged to the medium- and high-income groups, while the Flourishing category was dominated by the low- and medium-income groups. Similar to the 2016 QOL Survey, the Slight Lack of Flourishing and Lack of Flourishing categories were dominated by Singaporeans with low incomes in 2011.

Married Singaporeans were the majority in the High Flourishing and Flourishing categories, while there were more singles in the Slight Lack of Flourishing and Lack of Flourishing categories. In 2011, there were slightly more married Singaporeans in the High Flourishing category, while there were slightly more singles in the Very High Flourishing, Flourishing, and Slight Lack of Flourishing categories.

Conclusion

Over the past ten years (2006 to 2016), Singaporeans have become less happy, enjoyed life less, and felt a decreased sense of achievement. For the 2016 QOL Survey, most Singaporeans felt they had some control over their lives and a sense of purpose in life. It remains to be seen how this sense of control and purpose will change over time, together with the trends in the Happiness, Enjoyment and Achievement Indexes.

Education and household income had the most impact on Singaporeans' self- assessment of their happiness, enjoyment, achievement, control and purpose, while gender did not make any difference. Marital status was the next most impactful demographic variable, affecting Singaporeans' self-assessment of achievement, control and purpose. Age made a difference only when Singaporeans were self-assessing their achievements.

We have established good scale reliability for the 12-item Psychological Flourishing Scale and the 8-item Flourishing Scale. Using Diener and

Biswas-Diener's (2008) interpretation of the scores in the 12-item scale, Singaporeans seemed to have declined in Psychological Flourishing over the past five years from 2011 to 2016. Demographically, education, gender, household income and marital status contributed to differences in Singaporeans' assessment of their state of psychological flourishing.

References

AsiaBarometer Survey. www.asiabarometer.org (accessed January 10, 2017).

Blanchflower, D.G., and Oswald, A.J. (2000), *Well-being over time in Britain and the USA*, Cambridge, MA, USA: National Bureau of Economic Research.

Diener, E., and Biswas-Diener, R. (2008), *Happiness: Unlocking the mysteries of psychological wealth*, New York, NY, USA: Blackwell.

Diener, E., Gohm, C.L., Suh, E.M., and Oishi, S. (2000), 'Similarity of the relations between marital status and subjective well-being across cultures', *Journal of Cross-Cultural Psychology*, 31(4), 419–436.

Diener, E., Wirtz, D., Tov, W., Prieto, C.K., Choi, D., Oishi, S., and Biswas-Diener, R. (2010), 'New well-being measures: Short scales to assess flourishing and positive and negative feelings', *Social Indicators Research*, 97(2), 143–156.

Hone, L., Jarden, A., and Schofield, G. (2014), 'Psychometric properties of the flourishing scale in New Zealand', *Social Indicators Research*, published online November 6, 2013. DOI 10.1007/s11205-013-0501-x.

Inoguchi, T., and Fujii, S. (2009), 'The quality of life in Japan', *Social Indicators Research*, 92, 227–262.

Lee, G.R., Seccombe, K., and Shehan, C.L. (1991), 'Marital status and personal happiness: An analysis of trend data', *Journal of Marriage and the Family*, 53, 839–844.

Oswald, A.J. (1997), 'Happiness and economic performance', *Economic Journal*, 107(445), 1815–1831.

Ryan, R.M., and Deci, E.L. (2001), 'To be happy or to be self-fulfilled: A review of research on hedonic and eudaimonic wellbeing', in *Annual review of psychology*, edited by S. Fiske, Vol. 52, Palo Alto, CA, USA: Annual Reviews, 141–166.

Salama-Younes, M. (2017), 'Psychometric properties of the psychological flourishing scale in an Egyptian setting', *Journal of Psychology in Africa*, 27(4), 310–315.

Seligman, M. (2012), *Flourish: A visionary new understanding of happiness and wellbeing*, Hillsboro, OR, USA: Altraria Book.

Silva, A.J., and Caetano, A. (2013), 'Validation of the flourishing scale and scale of positive and negative experience in Portugal', *Social Indicators Research*, 110(2), 469–478.

Sumi, K. (2013), 'Reliability and validity of Japanese versions of the flourishing scale and the scale of positive and negative experience', *Social Indicators Research*, published online September 7, 2013. DOI 10.1007/s11205-013-0432-6.

Tambyah, S.K., and Tan, S.J. (2013), *Happiness and wellbeing: The Singaporean experience*, London, UK: Routledge.

Tambyah, S.K., Tan, S.J., and Kau, A.K. (2010), *The wellbeing of Singaporeans: Values, lifestyles, satisfaction and quality of life*, Singapore: World Scientific Publishing.

Tinkler, L., and Hicks, S. (2011), *Measuring subjective well-being*, London, UK: Office for National Statistics.

Veenhoven, R. (2012), 'Happiness also known as "life satisfaction" and "subjective well-being"', in *Handbook of social indicators and quality of life research*, edited by K.C. Land, A.C. Michalos and M.J. Sirgy, Dordrecht, Netherlands: Springer, 63–77.

Veroff, J., Douvan, E., and Kulka, R.A. (1981), *The inner American: A self-portrait from 1957 to 1976*, New York, NY, USA: Basic Books.

Villieux, A., Sovet, L., Jung, S.-C., and Guilbert, L. (2016), 'Psychological flourishing: Validation of the French version of the Flourishing Scale and exploration of its relationships with personality traits', *Personality and Individual Differences*, 88, 1–5.

4 Does money buy happiness in Singapore?

In our previous books, we have used household income as an independent variable in various data analyses, along with other demographics such as age, education, gender and marital status. We usually report the effect of household income on wellbeing outcomes such as happiness and life satisfaction. Invariably, the question will arise as to whether having more income or money makes anyone happier or more satisfied with her or his life. Like many people around the world, Singaporeans are curious about this question. It invites introspection and speculation about whether having more money does make a difference.

For this book, we decided to devote an entire chapter to the income–happiness debate. Although this debate has recently gained traction among the public at large, it is one that has been going on for years in academic circles. Before we go into the discussion, we highlight a selection of research studies that have investigated the intricate relationships among different types of income (e.g., actual incomes, relative incomes, etc.) and their influence on quality of life and wellbeing (e.g., happiness and life satisfaction). Many articles, books and commentaries have been written about the topic, although there are fewer publications specifically on Singapore and South East Asia. The amount of literature is overwhelming. To make the content more manageable, we have selected the research studies that may shed some light on the income–happiness equation for the Singaporean context. For those who are interested to explore further, several compilations of research studies focus on this issue. For instance, contributing authors to the *Handbook on the Economics of Happiness* (Bruni and Porta 2007) have provided analyses of the income–happiness paradox and theories for explaining the paradox (e.g., rising aspirations, positional externalities, the intrinsic and extrinsic nature of goals, etc.). Other books include *Recent Developments in the Economics of Happiness* (Frey and Stutzer 2013), *Happiness and Economic Growth: Lessons from Developing Countries* (Clark and Senik 2014) and *Consumer Economic Wellbeing* (Xiao 2015).

While we would like to provide comprehensive answers to every income–happiness question, we are working with the constraints of accessible data from both secondary sources and our primary QOL Survey datasets. To recap, for the 2016 QOL Survey, respondents were asked about their personal and household incomes. They were given the option not to disclose their incomes; thus the number of valid responses was smaller than the total sample size. We had 941 respondents for the question on monthly household income and a good spread across the income brackets. However, for monthly personal income, the number of respondents was 679, and there were very few respondents for the income brackets from S$9001 to more than S$20,000. Thus, we decided to run the data analyses using monthly household incomes. In this chapter, we discuss the relationship between household income and wellbeing outcomes such as happiness, enjoyment, achievement, control, purpose, satisfaction with life in general, satisfaction with overall quality of life and satisfaction with overall quality of life in Singapore. We also have measures about perceptions of economic wellbeing and how satisfied respondents were about their lives and life domains (e.g., income and standard of living). We will examine whether these related factors (such as financial satisfaction and satisfaction with standard of living) play a part in enhancing wellbeing.

Income and wellbeing outcomes

Wellbeing outcomes encompass both affective aspects (such as happiness and positive or negative affect) and cognitive aspects (such as life satisfaction). The need-fulfillment theory suggests that absolute income (or actual income) is important because money provides the resources to acquire the goods and services that contribute to one's happiness (Diener and Biswas-Diener 2002). Meeting needs leads to increased subjective wellbeing. A similar approach is the material desires concept where people will be happy to the extent that they can obtain things they desire or work/progress toward fulfilling these desires. Thus, on average, studies have shown that richer nations tended to be happier than poorer ones (e.g., Diener and Oishi 2000; Deaton 2013; Powdthavee et al. 2017).

Sengupta et al. (2012) found that household income had positive logarithmic associations with subjective QOL and happiness. Income seemed to be linked more strongly to people's evaluations of their life than to their happiness. The relationship between income and happiness also varied for different levels of income. The income–wellbeing association was strongest for people earning below the median income and tended to plateau for those in the upper quartile. In similar vein, Drakopoulos and Grimani (2013) showed that there was a strong positive relationship between income and happiness for low-income households and a nonsignificant relationship between income and happiness for high-income households. Their study was done using data from the European Foundation European Quality of Life Survey 2007, which contained data from 30 European countries and Turkey.

Income was negatively correlated to self-reported daily stress (Sengupta et al. 2012), a finding that was also discovered in Kushlev et al. (2015). Wealth may have a greater impact on sadness (negative affect), but it does not necessarily lead to more happiness (positive affect). They found that higher income was associated with experiencing less daily sadness, but had no effect on daily happiness. They concluded that "money may be a more effective tool for reducing sadness than enhancing happiness" (p. 488). Hudson et al. (2016) concurred that income reliably predicted daily sadness but not happiness. Income can help to reduce the sadness associated with everyday life but does not help to increase happiness.

The Easterlin Paradox

If income is positively impacting quality of life and wellbeing outcomes, this seems to suggest that nations and individuals should strive to be more materially prosperous. However, other theorists have counterargued that higher absolute incomes (or actual incomes) do not necessarily lead to higher levels of happiness, a phenomenon that has been termed the Easterlin Paradox. Easterlin (1974) first described this phenomenon when he noted that, over time, a higher rate of economic growth did not result in a greater increase in happiness. At a point in time, happiness and income were positively related, but over time within a country, happiness did not increase as income went up. He defended this position with data from more countries including developing countries, transitioning countries in Eastern Europe and a larger sample of developed countries (Easterlin et al. 2010). Despite phenomenal economic growth, wellbeing increased minimally even in the wealthier nations over the last few decades.

Ma and Zhang (2014) explained the Easterlin Paradox in terms of ecological correlation due to spatial aggregation or data grouping, change of reference classes and confounding variables. They proposed that happiness and income were correlated at the individual level but the correlation was not that strong. For nations, the correlation was stronger, contradicting the Easterlin Paradox. In examining countries that have experienced continuous income growth over an extended period of time, Clark et al. (2014) found an inverse relationship over time between GDP per capita and happiness inequality, where greater income per capita was associated with smaller standard deviations in happiness.

Various theories have been devised to explain the Easterlin Paradox. The key ones are related to concepts such as adaptation, social comparison and aspirations.

Adaptation

Increases in income contribute to happiness but only up to the level where basic needs are met (Diener and Selligman 2009). Thereafter, increases in income may not lead to increases in happiness. Thus, in wealthy countries, if basic needs are met, income ceases to be a good predictor of happiness (Diener and Oishi 2000). It seems that relative incomes (or perceived financial wellbeing) is a better predictor (Easterlin 1974; Oshio and Urakawa 2014). Beyond basic needs, people start comparing their incomes and make social comparisons about the satisfaction of higher-order needs (Drakopoulos 2013).

Another study has suggested a time lag for the levelling effect of income on happiness. Using three datasets on Germany, Di Telia and MacCulloch (2010) first provided evidence for full adaptation to economic growth after basic needs have been met. They showed that wealthier individuals (e.g., home owners) and countries adapted fully to higher levels of income (the logarithm of income) and GDP per capita (the logarithm of GDP per capita), respectively. However, these adaptations may take up to five years for countries and seven years for individuals. This suggests that the gains from happiness from higher income levels can be relatively long-lasting, though they are not for perpetuity.

Social comparison and aspirations

As mentioned earlier, once basic needs are met, additional income does little to raise one's sense of satisfaction with life. People adapt fairly quickly to a rise in income. Absolute income matters up to a certain point, but after that, relative income matters more. Relative income features prominently in social comparison (Festinger 1954). In terms of aspirations, it is suggested that the gap between income aspirations and actual income is a more important consideration for happiness (Michalos 1985). Materialistic values are also exerting an upward pressure on income aspirations, as desires race ahead of spending power.

Studies have found that relative incomes and income aspirations were significantly correlated to wellbeing (Huang et al. 2016; Knight and Gunatilaka 2011). Hagerty (2000) showed that the range and skew of the income distribution in a community affect a person's happiness as predicted by the range-frequency theory. This effect was also seen at the national level, where decreasing the skew of the income distribution in a country increased average national SWB. Perceptions about relative income (which is closely related to actual income) were highly correlated with happiness. People tended to compare with those who work in the same occupation and those who live in the same region. After controlling for own income and reference group income, higher perceptions about relative income predicted higher levels of happiness. Similarly, perceived social class was highly positively correlated with happiness (Guven and Sorensen 2012).

Yamashita et al. (2016) showed that relative income was a better predictor of happiness for East Asian countries such as China, Japan, South Korea and Taiwan. Huang et al. (2016) found that in urban China, absolute income had a positive association with happiness, while the reverse was true for relative income and happiness. Their research suggested policy implications for pro-poor growth, equal distribution for economic resources and asset-building policies as supplements to other social assistance programs.

Relative incomes can be "objectively measured" by using formulae such as the ratio of one's absolute income compared to the median income of the community one belongs to (e.g., country, province, neighbourhood, occupational group, etc.). Relative incomes have also been "subjectively measured" through perceptual scales with anchors such as "far above average" to "far below average." These scales are related to one's sense of financial wellbeing. People assess the adequacy of their incomes in relation to variable standards (i.e., relativistic judgement models, as mentioned in Diener and Oishi 2000). Ng (2015) found that material concerns had an indirect effect on the subjective wellbeing of Singaporeans. Specifically, financial satisfaction was one of the strongest predictors of life satisfaction and happiness. Ekici and Koydemir (2016) demonstrated that for UK households, subjective measures of current and future financial wellbeing were found to be significant correlates of life satisfaction, income satisfaction and mental health.

Using data from the Canadian National Population Health Survey (1994 to 2009), Latif (2016) examined the relationship between comparison income and individual happiness. Comparison income was defined in two ways: (1) the average income of the reference group and (2) the difference between one's own household income and the average income of the reference group. He found that an increase in the average income of the reference group reduced individual happiness. An individual was happier when his or her own household income grew compared to the average income of the reference group, even for different reference groups. In short, comparison income had a significant negative impact on an individual's happiness level.

Luo et al. (2016) showed that income aspirations were most important in explaining the variations in wellbeing, closely followed by absolute income. Relative income had the smallest effect. This emphasized the importance of aspirations and the prevailing climate of consumerism and materialism for determining wellbeing in China.

The undesirable effects of social comparison and income aspirations have been noted in studies as well. The behaviors associated with higher income such as longer work hours and the trade-offs of such hours for leisure, relationships and health have been shown to take a toll on the wellbeing of individuals and their families and communities. Despite economic growth, Chinese citizens were not happier (Li 2016). In addition to social comparison and (hedonic) adaptation, other factors were proposed. These include an expanding social capital deficit, environment pollution, growing social inequality and work–life imbalance due to the long working hours needed to obtain the desired income. Despite these pessimistic musings, Schnittker (2008) in his analysis of the General Social Survey data from 1973 to 2004 found that, generally, gains in real income were accompanied by enhanced financial satisfaction. Despite income inequality, perceptions of relative income had also increased. There was also no evidence for overworked families or individuals.

Income inequality

Another explanation suggests that income inequality or the distribution of income or wealth plays a critical role in how income is related to happiness. This effect can be seen even in relatively wealthy and developed countries. In recent years, this effect seems to be more pronounced in countries (e.g., China and Eastern European countries) that are transitioning from communism (a more socialist economic model) to capitalism (a market-based economic model). Studies have shown that economic growth and the attendant income increases in these countries were negatively associated with wellbeing because the gains from the transition were not equitably distributed (Oshio et al. 2011; Easterlin et al. 2012; Han 2015). Easterlin et al. (2012) noted that individual wellbeing in China was higher in 1990 when the people were less affluent overall but that income was relatively more equally distributed. Therefore, materialistic values could lower wellbeing, and policies to reduce the gap between expected incomes and actual incomes could effectively promote individuals' perceived wellbeing in China (Luo et al. 2016).

In an analysis of economic data from 34 countries, Oishi and Kesebir (2015) showed that economic growth did not lead to increases in happiness when it was accompanied by growing income equality. In terms of policy implications, they suggested that a more even distribution of national wealth may be a precondition for raising nationwide happiness.

Using the Chinese General Social Survey data, Wang et al. (2015) found that individual happiness increased with inequality when county-level inequality measured by the Gini coefficient was less than 0.405 and decreased with inequality for larger values of the Gini coefficient where approximately 60 percent of the countries in the study had a Gini coefficient of greater than 0.405. This implied that there was a range where individuals were prepared to accept some level of income inequality, beyond which happiness levels would be jeopardized.

The effects of income inequality on happiness are also mediated by other factors such as trust. Using the General Social Survey data in the United States from 1972 to 2008, Oishi et al. (2011) showed that in years of high income inequality, not only were Americans less happy, they trusted other people less and perceived other people to be less fair. This was especially so for respondents from lower-income households. The negative association between income inequality and happiness for lower-income respondents was explained not by lower household income but by perceived unfairness and lack of trust.

Methodological issues

As seen from past research, the relationship between income and happiness can be fairly complicated. Some complications are due to methodological issues, for example, the type and nature of income that is being assessed and the many measures of happiness that are used in various studies. As expounded by Clark (2011), the debate on income and happiness has been hampered by the lack of harmonized datasets across countries.

In a review of the income–happiness debate, Graham (2009) found the following: First, it matters which aspect of wellbeing is being measured. Studies have found that income affected evaluations of life satisfaction (cognitive aspect of wellbeing) but had minimal influence on positive affect (affective aspects of wellbeing). Second, it matters what questions are being asked and how they are phrased/framed. For instance, are the questions about affective aspects (e.g., smiling) or cognitive aspects (e.g., life satisfaction)? Are they general reference questions or framed reference (e.g., Cantril Ladder of Life) questions? And third, what is the specification of the income variable (e.g., absolute income, log income)? Graham (2009) concluded that "Income and wealth do a good job of explaining the distribution of responses on the ladder of life question . . . but they do not explain answers on smiling, life purpose and freedom to choose questions" (p. 35). She also found that education seemed to mediate the income–happiness relationship, where the least educated in poor countries and the more educated in both rich and poor countries had strong income–wellbeing links.

Using Gallup's extensive database, Diener et al. (2010) showed that GDP had a positive effect on life satisfaction but no effect on improvements in mood. This suggested an important distinction between material prosperity versus psychosocial prosperity. National income (GDP per capita) was the most important factor for general life satisfaction, but it was rather unimportant for the experience of positive or negative emotions. The experience of these emotions was reflected in the level of psychosocial prosperity (i.e., the extent to which people's social psychological needs were fulfilled). Increases in national income were accompanied by more favorable evaluations of life in general but not by substantial improvements in mood. Mood improvements seemed to occur only when psychosocial prosperity was enhanced through good social relationships, freedom of action and opportunities for personal development (Diener et al. 2010).

Happiness, enjoyment, achievement, control and purpose

Respondents in the 2016 QOL initially responded to the question on happiness, "All things considered, would you say that you are happy these days?" on a 5-point scale of "1 = very unhappy" to "5 = very happy." However, for consistency in analyses, we recoded the responses to a 4-point scale for parity with the questions on enjoyment, achievement, control and purpose. The recoding was done as follows: 1 and 2 were recoded as "1 = unhappy," 3 was recoded as "2 = neither happy nor unhappy," 4 was recoded as "3 = quite happy," and 5 was recoded as "4 = very happy." The question on enjoyment ("How often do you feel you are really enjoying life these days?") has a 4-point scale of "1 = never" to "4 = often," and the question on achievement ("How much do you feel you are accomplishing what you want out of life?") also has a 4-point scale of "1 = none" to "4 = a great deal." Respondents replied to the question on control ("How much control do you feel you have over important aspects of your life?") and the question on sense of purpose ("All things considered, how much do you feel you have a sense of purpose in your life?") on a 4-point scale of "1 = none" to "4 = a great deal."

Income and happiness

As shown in Figure 4.1 (dark gray line), Singaporeans' happiness level generally increases with income, except for two groups: those whose monthly household income falls into the range of (S$2001 to S$3000) and those in the range of (S$6001 to S$7000). The most notable point of inflection in this graph of happiness level is at the income range of (S$6001 to S$7000), which reported the steepest decrease and lowest level of happiness at 2.38 (out of a 4-point

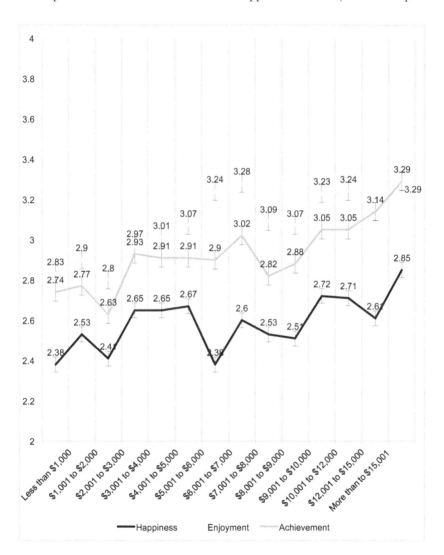

Figure 4.1 Happiness, enjoyment and achievement across household income levels (2016)

scale). This lowest point was also shared by those who were earning less than S$1000. The highest level of happiness (2.85) belonged to those from the highest income group (>S$20,000).

Income and enjoyment

As shown in Figure 4.1 (light gray line), Singaporeans' level of enjoyment generally increases as household income increases after a slight dip from 2.9 to 2.8 (out of a four-point scale) for those whose monthly household income falls into the range of S$2001 to S$3000. The first turning point in this upward trend occurred after the enjoyment level peaked at 3.28 (out of a 4-point sale) for those in the income range of S$7001 to S$8000, before gradually declining to 3.07 for the income range of S$9001 to S$10,000. Thereafter, the enjoyment level started to rise again before gradually declining to 3.14 for the income range of S$15,001 to S$20,000 and then finally increasing to a new high of 3.39 for the highest income group of more than S$20,000.

Income and achievement

As shown in Figure 4.1 (medium gray line), Singaporeans' level of accomplishment generally increases as household income increases after a slight dip from 2.77 to 2.63 (out of a 4-point scale) for those whose monthly household income falls into the range of S$2001 to S$3000. The first turning point in this upward trend occurred after the accomplishment level increased to 2.93 for those with household incomes in the range of S$3001 to S$4000, with the next point of inflection occurring at the income range of S$7001 to S$8000, with a higher level of accomplishment of 3.02. It then plunged to a level of 2.82 for the income range of S$8001 to S$9000. Thereafter, the level of accomplishment maintained its upward trend, reaching a new high level of 3.29 for Singaporeans in the highest household income group of more than S$20,000.

Income and control

As shown in Figure 4.2 (dark gray line), Singaporeans' level of control over important aspects of their life first showed an increase from the initial 2.69 (out of a 4-point scale) for those in the lowest income group (less than S$1000) to 2.86 for those in the income range of S$1001 to S$2000, followed by a slight decrease to 2.83 at the next income range of S$2001 to S$3000. Thereafter, the level of control goes on an upward trend until it reaches a high of 3.16 for the income range of S$7001 to S$8000. The first and only notable inflection point for the level of control trend occurred where there was a decline to 2. 93 for those who have household incomes in the range of S$9001 to S$10,000. Thereafter, the level of control began its upward trend, culminating with the highest level of control (3.29) for those with the highest income range of more than S$20,000.

out

of a 4-point scale) for those in the income range of

Income and sense of purpose

As shown in Figure 4.2 (light gray line), Singaporeans' sense of purpose in life generally showed a scallop-shaped pattern where the sense of purpose increases and alternates with decreases for the first few income ranges, until it reaches 3.19 (out of a 4-point scale) for those in the income range of S$5001 to S$6000. Thereafter, the sense of purpose began its gradual downward trend to a low of 2.98 for those in the income range of S$9001 to S$10,000, before increasing sharply to a high of 3.35 for those in the next income group of S$10,001 to S$15,000. This increase was not sustained as the level of sense of purpose then started to decrease for the next two income groups, before reaching the highest level of 3.39 for those in the highest income range of more than S$20,000.

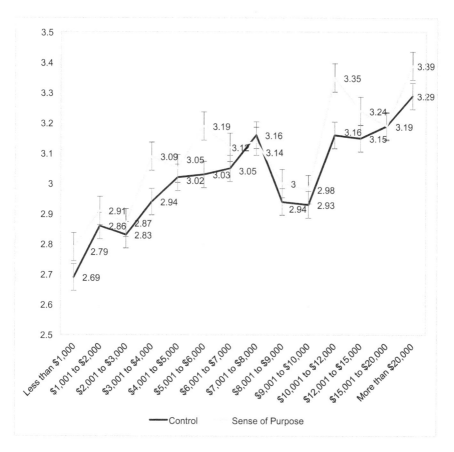

Figure 4.2 Control and sense of purpose across household income levels (2016)

Satisfaction with life, satisfaction with overall quality of life and satisfaction with overall quality of life in Singapore

Respondents in the survey were asked to rate their satisfaction with life on a 6-point scale ("'1 = strongly disagree" to "6 = strongly agree"). The five statements about satisfaction with life include "In most ways, my life is close to my ideal," "The conditions of my life are excellent," "I am satisfied with my life," "So far I have gotten the important things I want in life," and "If I could live my life over, I would change almost nothing." Each respondent's responses to these items were summed, and the average scores for these items were used in deriving the graph (dark gray line in Figure 4.3). Higher means thus indicated a greater degree of satisfaction.

For overall quality of life, respondents in the survey were asked to rate their satisfaction using a scale as follows: 1 for "very dissatisfied," 2 for "dissatisfied," 3 for "somewhat dissatisfied," 4 for "somewhat satisfied," 5 for "satisfied" and 6 for "very satisfied." A higher score thus indicated a greater degree of satisfaction.

Respondents in the survey were also asked to rate their satisfaction with overall quality of life in Singapore using a scale as follows: 1 for "very dissatisfied," 2 for "dissatisfied," 3 for "somewhat dissatisfied," 4 for "somewhat satisfied," 5 for "satisfied" and 6 for "very satisfied." Higher scores thus indicated a greater degree of satisfaction.

Income and satisfaction with life

As shown in Figure 4.3 (dark gray line), Singaporeans' satisfaction with life improved as income increased, from 4.03 (out of a 6-point scale) for those with less than S$1000 to 4.31 for those in the income group of S$5001 to S$6000. The first and most notable inflection point in the satisfaction with life trend occurred when the satisfaction level dropped sharply to 4.05 for those in the next income group S$6001 to S$7000, before rising to 4.3 for those in the next higher income group of S$7001 to S$8000. Then the satisfaction level again declined slightly to 4.11 for those in the next higher income group of S$8001 to S$9000, before starting on a gradual increase for the next few income groups, reaching the highest level of 4.45 for the highest-income group of more than S$20,000.

Income and satisfaction with overall quality of life

As shown in Figure 4.3 (light gray line), Singaporeans' satisfaction with overall quality of life improved as income increased, from 4.45 (out of a 6-point scale) for those with less than S$1000 to 4.77 for those in the income group of S$3001 to S$4000. The satisfaction level then started its slight downward slide for the next few income groups, reaching a level of 4.64 for the two income

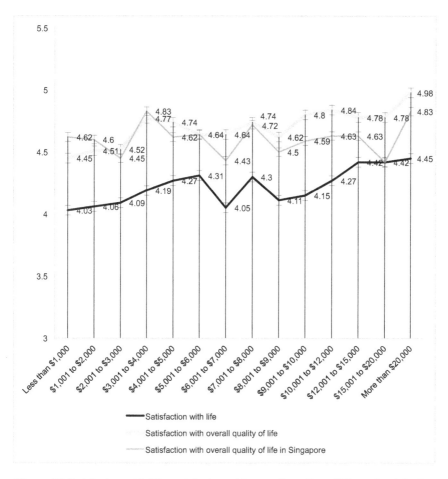

Figure 4.3 Satisfaction with life, satisfaction with overall quality of life, and satisfaction with overall quality of life in Singapore across household income levels (2016)

groups of S$5001 to S$6000 and S$6001 to S$7000, before increasing to 4.74 for those in the next higher income group of S$7001 to S$8000. Then the satisfaction level again declined to 4.62 for those in the next higher income group of S$8001 to S$9000, before starting on an upward path for the next few income groups, finally reaching the highest level of 4.98 for the highest-income group of more than S$20,000.

Income and satisfaction with overall quality of life in Singapore

As shown in Figure 4.3 (medium gray line), Singaporeans' satisfaction with overall quality of life in Singapore initially declined as income increased, from 4.62

Table 4.1 Correlations between wellbeing indicators and household incomes (2016)

Wellbeing indicators	Monthly household income[1]
Happiness	0.103[2]
Enjoyment	0.195[2]
Achievement	0.208[2]
Control	0.214[2]
Sense of purpose	0.219[2]
Satisfaction with life	0.122[2]
Satisfaction with life domains	0.152[2]
Satisfaction with living in Singapore	0.012

1 This analysis is based on responses from 941 respondents (out of total sample of 1503) who agreed to report on their household income.
2 Correlation is significant at 0.01 level.

(out of a 6-point scale) for the lowest-income group of less than S$1000 to 4.45 for those in the higher-income group of S$2001 to S$3000. The satisfaction level then increased sharply to 4.83 for those in the next higher income group of S$3001 to S$4000, before turning to a downward trend, decreasing to a new low of 4.43 for those in the S$6001–S$7000 income group. Satisfaction level then increased to 4.72 for the next higher income group of S$7001 to S$8000, before decreasing again to 4.45 for those in the next higher income group of S$8001 to S$9000. The next inflection point came when the satisfaction level dropped to its lowest of 4.42 for those in the income group of S$15,001 to S$20,000, before reaching the highest level of 4.83 for the highest-income group of more than S$20,000.

In addition to Figures 4.1 to 4.3, we examined correlations between household income and the wellbeing indicators. The correlations were all positive and ranged from 0.012 to 0.219, indicating that household income had an influence on the subjective wellbeing of Singaporeans. (See Table 4.1.)

Economic wellbeing

Economic wellbeing has been a subject of continuous debate and inquiry as researchers and policy makers try to answer the question, "Does money buy happiness?" Economic wellbeing is an overall assessment of how one feels about the adequacy of the resources available to her or him. A related concept would be financial wellbeing, which is defined as how much money one has to spend on oneself and which has been shown to contribute to one's overall wellbeing (Kruger 2010). Other related concepts would be financial satisfaction (i.e., how satisfied one is with the financial situation of one's household) and satisfaction with one's standard of living. Both of these material concerns were investigated by Ng and her colleagues using data from the World Values Survey (Ng 2015) and a Singapore-based survey conducted in 2017 (Ng et al. 2017). They found that financial satisfaction was one of the strongest predictors of life satisfaction and happiness. Similarly, our correlation analyses confirmed that satisfaction with household income (i.e., financial satisfaction) and satisfaction with standard of living were positively associated with the wellbeing indicators (See Table 4.2).

For the 2016 QOL Survey, we used three evaluative questions based on interval scales from the Gallup-Healthways Well-Being Index to measure economic wellbeing. One of the questions was modified to form the fourth question relating to the ability to service loan commitments. The responses to all four questions are indicated in Table 4.3. The numbers in parentheses indicate the percentages for the 2011 QOL Survey.

As shown in Table 4.3, eight out of ten (83.9 percent) Singaporeans in the 2016 QOL Survey agreed that they had enough money to buy the things they need, which was an improvement from 2011 (66.9 percent). Close to three-quarters (72.5 percent) of Singaporeans said they were able to meet loan repayments as planned. About six out of ten (61.4 percent) agreed that they had enough money to do what they wanted, compared to 32.5 percent in 2011. Slightly more than half (55.4 percent) mentioned that they did not have money to make a major purchase, which was also an improvement from 2011 (63.6 percent).

To see whether there are any individual differences, we further analyzed economic wellbeing by selected demographics and the results are presented in Tables 4.4 and 4.5. Almost equal percentages of male and female Singaporeans agreed that they had enough money to buy what they need, but a slightly higher percentage of single Singaporeans felt this way. Singaporeans in the youngest age group (15 to 24 years) had the highest percentage (88.6 percent) who felt they had enough money to buy the things they need, followed closely

Table 4.2 Correlations between satisfaction with household income and standard of living with wellbeing indicators (2016)[1]

Wellbeing indicators	Satisfaction with household income	Satisfaction with standard of living
Happiness	0.460[2]	0.420[2]
Enjoyment	0.349[2]	0.397[2]
Achievement	0.435[2]	0.395[2]
Control	0.375[2]	0.335[2]
Sense of purpose	0.344[2]	0.333[2]
Satisfaction with life	0.643[2]	0.587[2]
Satisfaction with overall quality of life	0.596[2]	0.599[2]
Satisfaction with overall quality of life in Singapore	0.403[2]	0.474[2]

1 These correlations are based on responses from the total sample population of 1503 Singapore citizens.
2 Correlation is significant at 0.01 level.

Table 4.3 Singaporeans' economic wellbeing scores (2016 QOL Survey)

Do you/your household have enough money to buy the things you need?		If you/your household have/has a loan, are you/your household able to meet these monthly/regular commitments as planned?	
(1) Yes, have enough (%)	(2) No, do not have enough (%)	(1) Yes, have enough (%)	(2) No, do not have enough (%)
83.9 (66.9)	16.1 (33.1)	72.5 (N.A.)	27.5 (N.A.)

Do you/your household have more than enough money to do what you want to do?		Would you/your household be able to make a major purchase, such as a car, appliance or furniture, or pay for a significant home repair if you needed to?	
(1) Agree (%)	(2) Disagree (%)	(1) Yes, would be able to (%)	(2) No, would not be able to (%)
61.4 (32.5)	38.6 (67.5)	44.6 (36.4)	55.4 (63.6)

N.A. = Not available.

Table 4.4 Demographic distribution of "Do you/your household have enough money to buy the things you need?"

Demographics	Have enough money to buy things you need (%)	Don't have enough money to buy things you need (%)
Total sample	83.9	16.1
Age groups (years)		
• 15–24	88.6	11.4
• 25–34	80.9	19.1
• 35–44	83.5	16.5
• 45–54	80.3	19.7
• 55–64	87.7	12.3
• 65 and above	83.5	16.5
Education		
• Low	75.2	24.8
• Medium	81.7	18.3
• High	92.7	7.3
Gender		
• Male	85.9	14.1
• Female	81.9	18.1
Household income		
• Low	67.1	32.9
• Medium-low	85.1	14.9
• Medium-high	95.2	4.8
• High	93.3	6.7
Marital status		
• Single	86.7	13.3
• Married	83.9	16.1

(87.7 percent) by those in the retiring age group (55 to 64 years). Not surprisingly, more among the less educated and lower-income Singaporeans felt that they did not have enough money to buy the things they needed. More among the single Singaporeans felt that they had enough money to buy what they need.

Table 4.5 shows that Singaporeans were generally able to meet their monthly loan commitments (if they had any) except for those in the oldest age group (65 years and above), where only about half (54.3 percent) said that they were able to meet such commitments. More education and house-hold income also helped Singaporeans in their ability to meet their loan commitments. Females seemed to lag behind males in their ability to service loan commitments, while married Singaporeans had less ability to do so than singles.

Table 4.6 shows that Singaporeans' financial ability to do the things they want to do improved as they get older, especially for those in the 55- to 64-year

Table 4.5 Demographic distribution of "If you/your household have/has a loan, are you/your household able to meet these monthly/regular commitments as planned?"

Demographics	Have enough money (%)	Don't have enough money (%)
Total sample	72.5	27.5
Age groups (years)		
• 15–24	75.7	24.3
• 25–34	72.8	27.2
• 35–44	77.2	22.8
• 45–54	75.7	24.3
• 55–64	74.1	25.9
• 65 and above	54.3	45.7
Education		
• Low	40.4	59.6
• Medium	70.2	29.8
• High	92.7	7.3
Gender		
• Male	75.3	24.7
• Female	69.8	30.2
Household income		
• Low	42.9	57.1
• Medium-low	79.3	20.7
• Medium-high	95.5	4.5
• High	97.1	2.9
Marital status		
• Single	75.4	24.6
• Married	73.0	27.0

Table 4.6 Demographic distribution of "Do you/your household have more than enough money to do what you want to do?"

Demographics	Have enough money for wants (%)	Don't have enough money for wants (%)
Total sample	61.4	38.6
Age groups (years)		
• 15–24	57.8	42.2
• 25–34	56.1	43.9
• 35–44	61.5	38.5
• 45–54	60.1	39.9
• 55–64	68.3	31.7
• 65 and above	64.6	35.4
Education		
• Low	50.3	49.7
• Medium	58.2	41.8
• High	73.6	26.4
Household income		
• Low	41.7	58.3
• Medium-low	60.3	39.7
• Medium-high	77.4	22.6
• High	80.6	19.4
Gender		
• Male	63.5	36.5
• Female	59.3	40.7
Marital status		
• Single	59.7	40.3
• Married	63.0	37.0

age group. More education and household income also helped Singaporeans in their financial ability to do what they want. Females seemed to have less discretionary purchasing power in this area than males.

Table 4.7 shows that middle-aged Singaporeans (35 to 44 years old) were the majority who could afford to make a major purchase any time they want, while retirees (those aged 65 years and above) formed the majority who could not afford to make such impromptu purchases. As Singaporeans' education and income levels increase, the percentages who felt they were able to make a major purchase also increased. However, there were no gender differences where ability to make a major purchase was concerned, with about five out of ten (54.5 and 56.2 percent) of both genders admitting that they did not have enough money to do so. The same pattern of responses applied to marital status.

Table 4.7 Demographic distribution of "Would you/your household be able right now to make a major purchase such as a car, appliance, or furniture or pay for a significant home repair if you needed to?"

Demographics	Yes, able to make major purchase (%)	No, not able to make major purchase (%)
Total sample	44.6	55.4
Age groups (years)		
• 15–24	44.6	55.4
• 25–34	41.6	58.4
• 35–44	51.9	48.1
• 45–54	48.6	51.4
• 55–64	44.8	55.2
• 65 and above	32.0	68.0
Education		
• Low	23.0	77.0
• Medium	38.3	61.7
• High	68.3	31.7
Gender		
• Male	45.5	54.5
• Female	43.8	56.2
Household income		
• Low	17.7	82.3
• Medium-low	43.5	56.5
• Medium-high	70.6	29.4
• High	85.1	14.9
Marital status		
• Single	44.1	55.9
• Married	46.6	53.4

Conclusion

Money does seem to buy happiness as our data showed a general trend that happiness increased as household incomes increased (see Figure 4.1). However, there were exceptions where Singaporeans in the higher-income group (S$6001 to S$7000) may not be happier than those in the lower-income group (S$2001 to S$3000). In terms of the level of enjoyment, although Singaporeans who did not enjoy life as much mostly belonged to the lower-income groups, those in the middle-low income group (S$7001 to S$8000) can have the same high enjoyment level as those in the highest household income group (>S$20,000). Although household income had a positive relationship with Singaporeans' ability to accomplish what they want in life, there were again exceptions where people with higher income (S$8001 to S$9000) reported lower levels of accomplishment than those with lesser income (S$7001 to S$8000).

Income does matter in Singaporeans' level of control over important aspects of their lives, as it generally improved as income increased, but there were again exceptions (see Figure 4.2). Singaporeans who had higher household incomes (such as those in the S$8001 to S$9000 and S$9001 to S$10,000 ranges) may not feel that they had more control than their fellow citizens in the lower-income groups. As far as Singaporeans' sense of purpose was concerned, income had the same impact as it had on control: It improved as income increased but with exceptions. Singaporeans with high household incomes in the ranges of S$8001 to S$9000, S$9001 to S$10,000, and S$15,001 to S$20,000 may not have a higher sense of purpose than their fellow citizens in the lower-income groups.

Income also had a positive relationship with Singaporeans' satisfaction with life, although one can have higher income but be not really satisfied with life (see Figure 4.3). This is particularly so for those in the middle-low income group (S$6001 to S$7000) who could have similar low satisfaction levels as those in the lowest-income group (<S$1000). Meanwhile, once Singaporeans' household incomes passed the S$15,000 mark, their satisfaction with life may not increase substantially as their income increased. Apart from the lowest- and highest-income groups, satisfaction with the overall quality of life may not increase with higher household incomes. Singaporeans in the lower-income group of S$3001 to S$4000 can have a higher satisfaction level than their fellow citizens with higher incomes (from S$4001 to S$9000).

Similarly, although income had a generally positive relationship with Singaporeans' satisfaction with overall quality of life in Singapore, one can have higher income but be not really satisfied with living in Singapore. Even Singaporeans with less than S$1000 can have higher satisfaction than those with higher incomes, especially when compared with those in the middle-income (S$6001 to S$7000) and high-income (S$15,001 to S$20,000) groups.

In terms of buying items of basic needs, meeting obligatory payments, and doing things they want to do, Singaporeans were economically well-off. A large majority (more than 60 percent) of Singaporeans were able to meet these needs in 2016, and the percentages were generally more than those reported in 2011. When it comes to making a major purchase like a car or a home appliance or paying for significant home repairs, many Singaporeans (55.5 percent) were still unable to do so. However, this was an improvement compared to 2011 (63.6 percent).

Who were the Singaporeans who were doing well or not doing so well economically? For buying items for basic needs, the youngest age group (15 to 24 years) and the retiring age group (55 to 64 years) were most able to do so, while the young working adults age group (25 to 34 years) and the middle-aged group (45 to 54 years) were less able to do so. Those with low levels of education and correspondingly low household incomes were least able to meet such needs. Male and female Singaporeans, whether single or married, were equally comfortable with paying for such needs. Singaporeans who were above 65 years of age, those with low levels of education, and those with low household incomes were least able to meet monthly commitments as planned. Gender and marital status did not distinguish Singaporeans on this commitment ability.

Young Singaporeans (15 to 34 years), those with low levels of education, and those with low household incomes were less able to have money to do what they want. Again, gender and marital status did not distinguish Singaporeans on their ability to afford the things they wanted. When making a major purchase like a car or a household appliance or paying for major home repairs, retirees (65 years and above) were least able to do so (68 percent compared to the national average of 55.4 percent), followed by those with low levels of education (77 percent) and those with low household incomes (82.3 percent).

Overall, Singaporeans were generally doing well in terms of economic wellbeing. However, depending on the nature of the financial needs, some segments of Singaporeans may not be economically well-off. Many of them were likely to be older and had lower levels of education and correspondingly low household incomes.

Do the Easterlin Paradox and related theories apply to Singapore? Singapore is a well-to-do society with a robust GDP and a high standard of living. In the Singaporean context, it is possible that some of the theories mentioned earlier are working in tandem to influence the relationship between income and happiness. Absolute or actual incomes matter in Singapore, as it is becoming more expensive to maintain a good standard of living given the rising costs of living. Relative incomes play a part because of the strong peer pressure to keep up with one's reference groups (e.g., relatives, close friends, colleagues and neighbors). Aspirations also fuel the competitive striving for more income and the status that comes with having access to more resources. Income inequality could also adversely affect the wellbeing of and trust among citizens if the economic gains were not perceived to be equitably distributed.

References

Bruni, L., and Porta, P.L. (2007), *Handbook on the economics of happiness*, Cheltenham, UK: Edward Elgar.

Clark, A.E. (2011), 'Income and happiness: Getting the debate straight', *Applied Research in Quality of Life*, 6, 253–263.

Clark, A.E., Fleche, S., and Senik, C. (2014), 'The great happiness moderation: Well-being inequality during episodes of income growth', in *Happiness and economic growth: Lessons from developing countries*, edited by A. Clark and C. Senik, New York, NY, USA: Oxford University Press, 32–86.

Clark, A.E., and Senik, C. (2014), *Happiness and economic growth: Lessons from developing countries*, Oxford, UK: Oxford University Press.

Deaton, A. (2013), 'Income, health, and well-being around the world: Evidence from the Gallup World Poll', in *Recent developments in the economics of happiness*, edited by B. Frey and A. Stutzer, Northampton, MA, USA: Edward Elgar, 342–361.

Diener, E., and Biswas-Diener, R. (2002), 'Will money increase subjective wellbeing? A literature review and guide to needed research', *Social Indicators Research*, 57, 119–169.

Diener, E., Ng, W., Harter, J., and Arora, R. (2010), 'Wealth and happiness across the world: Material prosperity predicts life evaluation, whereas psychosocial prosperity predicts positive feeling', *Journal of Personality and Social Psychology*, 99(1), 52–61.

Diener, E., and Oishi, S. (2000), 'Money and happiness: Income and subjective well-being across nations', in *Culture and subjective well-being*, edited by E. Diener and E. Suh, Cambridge, MA, USA: MIT Press, 185–218.

Diener, E. and Selligman, M.P. (2009), 'Beyond money: Toward an economy of wellbeing', in *The science of wellbeing*, edited by E. Diener, Vol. 37, Dordrecht, Netherlands: Springer, 201–265.

Di Telia, R., and MacCulloch, R. (2010), 'Happiness adaptation to income beyond "basic needs"', in *International differences in well-being*, edited by E. Diener, J.F. Helliwell and D. Kahneman, New York, NY, USA: Oxford University Press, 217–246.

Drakopoulos, S.A. (2013), 'Hierarchical needs, income comparisons, and happiness levels', in *A positive psychology perspective on quality of life*, edited by A. Efklides and D. Moraitou, New York, NY, USA: Springer Science + Business Media, 17–32.

Drakopoulos, S.A., and Grimani, K. (2013), 'Maslow's needs hierarchy and the effect of income on happiness levels', in *The happiness compass: Theories, actions and perspectives for well-being*, edited by F. Sarracino, Hauppauge, NY, USA: Nova Science, 295–309.

Easterlin, R.A. (1974), *Does economic growth improve the human lot? Some empirical evidence in nations and households in economic growth*, New York, NY, USA: Academic Press.

Easterlin, R.A., McVey, L.A., Switek, M., Sawangfa, O., and Zweig, J.S. (2010), 'The happiness-income paradox revisited', *Proceedings of the National Academy of Sciences*, 107(52), 22243–22468.

Easterlin, R.A., Morgan, R., Switek, M., and Wang, F. (2012), 'China's life satisfaction, 1990–2010', *Proceedings of the National Academy of Sciences of the United States of America*, 109(25), 9775–9780.

Ekici, T., and Koydemir, S. (2016), 'Income expectations and happiness: Evidence from British panel data', *Applied Research in Quality of Life*, 11(2), 539–552.

Festinger, L. (1954), 'A theory of social comparison processes', *Human Relations*, 7, 117–140.

Frey, B.S., and Stutzer, A. (2013), *Recent developments in the economics of happiness*, Cheltenham, UK: Edward Elgar.

Graham, C. (2009), 'The happiness and income debate: Substance, methodology, and the Easterlin Paradox', in *Happiness around the world: The paradox of happy peasants and miserable millionaires*, Oxford, UK: Oxford University Press, 24–45.

Guven, C., and Sorensen, B.E. (2012), 'Subjective wellbeing: Keeping up with the perception of the Joneses', *Social Indicators Research*, 109, 439–469.

Hagerty, M.R. (2000), 'Social comparisons of income in one's community: Evidence from national surveys of income and happiness', *Journal of Personality and Social Psychology*, 78, 764–771.

Han, C. (2015), 'Explaining the subjective wellbeing of urban and rural Chinese: Income, personal concerns and societal evaluations', *Social Science Research*, 49, 179–190.

Huang, J., Wu, S., and Deng, S. (2016), 'Relative income, relative assets, and happiness in urban China', *Social Indicators Research*, 126, 971–985.

Hudson, N.W., Lucas, R.E., Donnellan, M.B., and Kushlev, K. (2016), 'Income reliably predicts daily sadness, but not happiness: A replication and extension of Kushlev, Dunn, and Lucas (2015)', *Social Psychological and Personality Science*, 7, 828–836.

Knight, J., and Gunatilaka, R. (2011), 'Great expectations? The subjective wellbeing of rural-urban migrants in China', *Oxford Development Studies*, 39(1), 1–24.

Kruger, P.S. (2010), 'Wellbeing: The five essential elements', *Applied Research in Quality of Life*, 6(3), 325–328.

Kushlev, K., Dunn, E.W., and Lucas, R.E. (2015), 'Higher income is associated with less daily sadness but not more daily happiness', *Social Psychological and Personality Science*, 6, 483–489.

Latif, E. (2016), 'Happiness and comparison income: Evidence from Canada', *Social Indicators Research*, 128, 161–177.

Li, J.Y. (2016), 'Why economic growth did not translate to increased happiness: Preliminary results of a multilevel modeling of happiness in China', *Social Indicators Research*, 128, 241–263.

Luo, Y., Wang, T., and Huang, X. (2016), 'Which types of income matter most for wellbeing in China: Absolute, relative or income aspirations?', *International Journal of Psychology*. DOI 10.1002/ijop.12284 (accessed December 4, 2017).

Ma, Y.Z., and Zhang, Y. (2014), 'Resolution of the happiness-income paradox', *Social Indicators Research*, 119, 705–721.

Michalos, A.C. (1985), 'Multiple discrepancies theory (MDT)', *Social Indicators Research*, 16(4), 347–413.

Ng, W. (2015), 'Processes underlying links to subjective wellbeing: Material concerns, autonomy and personality', *Journal of Happiness Studies*, 16, 1575–1591.

Ng, W., Kang, S., and Kua, W. (2017), 'What determines subjective well-being in Singapore? The importance of personality, financial satisfaction, and psychological needs', manuscript under review.

Oishi, S., and Kesebir, S. (2015), 'Income inequality explains why economic growth does not always translate to an increase in happiness', *Psychological Science*, 26, 1630–1638.

Oishi, S., Kesebir, S., and Diener, E. (2011), 'Income inequality and happiness', *Psychological Science*, 22, 1095–1100.

Oshio, T., Nozaki, K., and Kobayashi, M. (2011), 'Relative income and happiness in Asia: Evidence from nationwide surveys in China, Japan, and Korea', *Social Indicators Research*, 104, 351–367.

Oshio, T., and Urakawa, K. (2014), 'The association between perceived income inequality and subjective wellbeing: Evidence from a social survey in Japan', *Social Indicators Research*, 116, 755–770.

Powdthavee, N., Burkhauser, R.V., and De Neve, J. (2017), 'Top incomes and human well-being: Evidence from the Gallup World Poll', *Journal of Economic Psychology*, 62, 246–257.

Schnittker, J. (2008), 'Diagnosing our national disease: Trends in income and happiness, 1973 to 2004', *Social Psychology Quarterly*, 71(3), 257–280.

Sengupta, N.K., Osborne, D., Houkamau, C.A., Hoverd, W.J., Wilson, M.S., and Halliday, L.M. (2012), 'How much happiness does money buy? Income and subjective well-being in New Zealand', *New Zealand Journal of Psychology*, 41(2), 21–34.

Wang, P., Pan, J., and Luo, Z. (2015), 'The impact of income inequality on individual happiness: Evidence from China', *Social Indicators Research*, 121, 413–435.

Xiao, J.J. (2015), *Consumer economic wellbeing*, New York, NY, USA: Springer.

Yamashita, T., Bardo, A., and Liu, D. (2016), 'Are East Asians happy to work more or less? Associations between working hours, relative income and happiness in China, Japan, South Korea and Taiwan', *Asian Journal of Social Psychology*, 19, 264–274. G16.

5 Values and their influence on Singaporeans' subjective wellbeing

Values and their impact on behaviors and wellbeing outcomes have been a fruitful area of research in the social sciences. During the 1960s and 1970s, Rokeach (1968, 1973) asserted that values was an important component of the research on culture, society, social attitudes and behavior. In his research on lifestyles, Mitchell (1983, p. vii) defined values as "the whole constellation of a person's attitudes, beliefs, opinions, hopes, fears, prejudices, needs, desires, and aspirations that, taken together, govern how one behaves." Values premised on religious beliefs also have a significant influence on individuals and communities.

Many country-level and region-level studies (e.g., The European Social Survey and our QOL Surveys in Singapore) have incorporated measures on values in their data collection. One of the largest studies related to values is the World Values Survey, a global network of social scientists that has been studying changing values and their impact on social and political life since 1981. To date, more than 400 publications using the World Values Survey (WVS) have contributed substantially to our understanding of how value systems influence various aspects of our lives. Similar to previous waves, the questionnaire for the most recent WVS Wave 7 data collection comprises 290 questions and measures "cultural values, attitudes and beliefs towards gender, family, and religion, attitudes and experience of poverty, education, health, and security, social tolerance and trust, attitudes towards multilateral institutions, cultural differences and similarities between regions and societies" and includes new topics such as "justice, moral principles, corruption, accountability and risk, migration, national security and global governance."

Researchers have conceptualized and developed various measures on values for use in these large-scale surveys. For the 2016 QOL Survey, we used the List of Values (Kahle 1983, 1996) and the Portrait Values Questionnaire (Schwartz 2007). The List of Values (LOV) measure has been used in many contexts and "a large body of research has documented its reliability and validity" (Stockard et al. 2014, p. 230). The Portrait Values Questionnaire (PVQ) (Schwartz 2007) is also an established scale that has been validated and widely used (e.g., in the World Values Survey and many other studies).

In this chapter, we assess the importance of certain personal values to Singaporeans and specific demographic groups by age, gender, education, monthly household income and marital status. In addition to tracking changes in the LOV over time, we also conduct regression analyses to examine the impact of the values in the LOV and the PVQ on Singaporeans' subjective wellbeing.

List of values

In this section, we examine how Singaporeans felt about some personal values using the LOV. There are nine items in this measure: (1) Sense of Belonging, (2) Security, (3) Self-respect, (4) Warm Relationships with Others, (5) Fun and Enjoyment in Life, (6) Being Well-respected, (7) Sense of Accomplishment, (8) Self-fulfillment, and (9) Excitement (see Table 5.1).

In Singapore, the LOV was used in nationwide surveys conducted in 1996, 2001, 2011 and 2016. In all four surveys, respondents were asked to rate the nine values in the LOV on a 6-point scale ("1 = not important at all"; "6 = very important"). The mean score of each value was used to rank the values from the most important to the least. The 1996 survey was conducted by a reputable market research agency, using a stratified random sampling approach, resulting in a total of 1525 valid responses. The sample was found to be biased toward younger and more educated individuals and underrepresented older and less educated individuals. To achieve representativeness of the national population, the sample was weighted by age and education using the 1995 Census data (see Kau et al. 1998). Hence for this analysis, we used the weighted sample for 1996 data. The 2001 survey was similarly conducted by a profes-sional research agency using the same stratified random sampling approach.

Table 5.1 List of values

Value	Description
Sense of belonging	To be accepted and needed by your family, friends, and community.
Security	To be safe and protected from misfortune and attack.
Self-respect	To be proud of yourself and confident with who you are.
Warm relationships with others	To have close companionships and intimate friendships.
Fun and enjoyment in life	To lead a pleasurable life.
Being well-respected	To be admired by others and to receive recognition.
Sense of accomplishment	To succeed at whatever you do.
Self-fulfillment	To find peace of mind and to make the best use of your talents.
Excitement	To experience stimulation and thrills.

Source: Kahle (1996)

The final sample of 1500 was found to be representative of the national population (see Kau et al. 2004). The 2011 and 2016 QOL Surveys were conducted by the same agency that conducted the 2001 survey, and the final samples of 1500 and 1503 (respectively) were similarly found to be representative of the national population. In the 1996 and 2001 surveys, the LOV was administered to both Singapore citizens and Permanent Residents, whereas in the 2011 and 2016 QOL Surveys, only Singapore citizens responded to the survey. Hence, for comparison, only responses of Singapore citizens were considered in the analyses across demographic groups. The nationally representative samples of the 1996 (weighted), 2001, 2011 and 2016 surveys enabled us to do the comparisons across time.

General comparisons for choices and ranks

In Table 5.2a and Table 5.2b, we report the percentages of respondents who picked a particular value as "important" or "very important." As shown in the tables, there were changes in the choice of important values over the past two decades. However, no definite positive or negative trend was observed. Comparing 2001 with 1996 data (see Table 5.2a), all but one value declined in importance, with Security having the largest drop in importance. The only value that had a positive trend was Excitement. Comparing 2011 with 1996 data (see Table 5.2a), the upswing for Excitement continued, while the negative trend for some values was reversed. For instance, Warm Relationships with Others, Sense of Accomplishment, Self-fulfillment, Sense of Belonging, and Fun and Enjoyment achieved increases in importance. Comparing 2011 data with 2001 data revealed a different trend (see Table 5.2a). All values showed a positive improvement in importance except for Excitement, which showed a decline in importance. Sense of Belonging registered the largest percentage increase in importance, followed by Security.

Comparing the 2016 data with those of 1996, 2001 and 2011 data (see Table 5.2b), no definite positive or negative trend was observed, but some changes were notable. Comparing 2016 and 1996 data, we noticed that Being Well-respected had been given less emphasis (5.6 percent decrease in responses that the value is considered "important" and "very important") over the past 20 years, while Self-fulfillment has been given more consideration (11 percent increase). Comparing 2016 against 2001 data, it appeared that Security had been given much greater emphasis (25 percent increase in responses that the value is "important" and "very important"), while Excitement had been given lesser emphasis (8.4 percent decrease). Comparing 2016 against 2011 data, Security continued to be given more importance (6.2 percent increase), while Excitement continued its decline in importance (7.4 percent decrease).

Despite the absence of significant trends in the choice of important values over the past two decades, the rankings of the values' importance means did reveal some interesting insights (see Table 5.3). A higher mean indicates that a particular value is considered more important. The top three values have seen

Table 5.2a List of values for the 1996, 2001 and 2011 QOL Surveys

List of values	1996 survey (%)[1] Singapore citizens only (N = 1438)	2001 survey (%)[1] Singapore citizens only (N = 1378)	% change compared to 1996 (Singapore citizens only)	2011 survey (%)[1] Singapore citizens only (N = 1500)	% change compared to 1996 (Singapore citizens only)	% change compared to 2001 (Singapore citizens only)
Self-respect	86.7	70.3	-16.4	82.3	-4.4	+12.0
Security	86.3	65.9	**-20.4**	84.7	-1.6	+18.8
Being well-respected	76.9	67.2	-9.7	71.7	**-5.2**	+4.5
Warm relationships with others	76.6	70.8	-5.8	82.2	+5.6	+11.4
Sense of accomplishment	72.5	65.2	-7.3	75.5	+3.0	+10.3
Self-fulfillment	68.9	67.9	-1.0	76.9	+8.0	+9.0
Sense of belonging	72.2	57.8	-14.4	81.5	+9.3	**+23.7**
Fun and enjoyment	67.4	62.3	-5.1	73.1	+5.7	+10.8
Excitement	40.1	53.5	**+13.4**	52.5	**+12.4**	-0.9

1 Percentages reported in this table combine "important" and "very important" ratings.

Bold figures indicate largest positive or negative changes.

Table 5.2b List of values for the 2016 QOL Survey

List of values	2016 survey (%)[1]			
	Singapore citizens only (N = 1503)	% Change compared to 1996 (Singapore citizens only)	% Change compared to 2001 (Singapore citizens only)	% Change compared to 2011 (Singapore citizens only)
Self-respect	85.8	−0.9	+15.5	+3.5
Security	90.9	+4.6	**+25**	**+6.2**
Being well-respected	71.3	**−5.6**	+4.1	−0.4
Warm relationships with others	84.3	+7.7	+13.5	+2.1
Sense of Accomplishment	74.1	+1.6	+8.9	−1.4
Self-fulfillment	79.9	**+11**	+12	+3
Sense of belonging	82.1	+9.9	+24.3	+0.6
Fun and enjoyment	72.1	+4.7	+9.8	−1
Excitement	45.1	+5	−8.4	**−7.4**

1 Percentages reported in this table combine "important" and "very important" ratings.

Bold figures indicate largest positive or negative changes.

Table 5.3 List of values (ranking of importance means)

List of values	1996 (rank)	2001 (rank)	2011 (rank)	2016 (rank)
Self-respect	5.40 (1)	4.83 (1)	5.03 (2)	5.06 (2)
Security	5.28 (2)	4.72 (5)	5.09 (1)	5.19 (1)
Being well-respected	5.10 (3)	4.77 (3)	4.88 (7)	4.75 (8)
Warm relationships with others	5.08 (4)	4.83 (1)	4.99 (3)	5.02 (3)
Sense of accomplishment	4.94 (5)	4.70 (6)	4.90 (6)	4.82 (6)
Self-fulfillment	4.83 (6)	4.76 (4)	4.93 (5)	4.93 (5)
Sense of belonging	4.94 (7)	4.60 (8)	4.98 (4)	4.97 (4)
Fun and enjoyment	4.79 (8)	4.65 (7)	4.85 (8)	4.80 (7)
Excitement	4.01 (9)	4.49 (9)	4.44 (9)	4.14 (9)

Note: Means of scale ranging from "1 = Not important at all" to "6 = Very important."

some changes over the past 20 years. In 1996, the top three values were Self-respect, Security and Being Well-respected. However, five years later (2001), Self-respect and Warm Relationships with Others both became top ranked, followed by Being Well-respected, while Security was ranked 5th. Ten years later in 2011, Security became the most important value, followed by Self-respect and Warm Relationships with Others. Being Well-respected, which was ranked 3rd in 1996 and 2001, became less important and ranked 7th out of nine values. Five years later in 2016, the top two values remained the same as those in 2011, but Being Well-respected further declined to being ranked 8th out of nine values. Another noticeable change in ranking over the past 20 years is that Sense of Belonging has improved in rank, from being ranked 7th and 8th in 1996 and 2001 respectively, to 4th in 2011 and 2016. Some consistency is also being observed in Singaporeans' ranking of the importance of the nine values, with Fun and Enjoyment being ranked either 7th or 8th, and Excitement always ranked last over the past 20 years.

Using a translated version of the LOV, Grunert and Scherhorn's (1990) study in West Germany found that Sense of Belonging was rated highest in importance among the 1008 subjects surveyed, followed closely by Security. Self-fulfillment and Excitement were ranked second to last and last in importance. Their results were similar to our 1996 survey as far as the lowest-ranked value of Excitement, lower-ranked (6th) value of Self-fulfillment and 2nd-ranked value of Security were concerned, except for Sense of Belonging which was ranked 7th by Singaporeans.

In their study of changes in social values in the United States over 30 years from 1976 to 2007, Gurel-Atay et al. (2010) found that values such as Self-respect, Fun and Enjoyment, and Excitement showed the greatest gain in importance, with Self-respect as the most important value in 2007. Warm Relationships with Others and Self-fulfillment were close seconds in order of importance. The values of Security and Sense of Belonging demonstrated the most decline in importance. They also found that there was a reverse pattern in importance placed on different values; more important values in 1986 were perceived as less important in 2007. Their results contrasted with what we have found in the three surveys between the years 1996 and 2011 (Tambyah and Tan 2013). In Singapore, Fun and Enjoyment and Excitement have consistently been ranked last or second to last among the nine values over the three periods, while Security and Sense of Belonging have risen to top positions over this period. However, like the Americans, Singaporeans valued Self-respect, Warm Relationships with Others and Self-fulfillment over the years 1996 to 2011.

Sources of individual differences in LOV

Age

As shown in the second column of Table 5.4, age had a negative and significant correlation with all nine values in LOV, implying that older Singaporeans regarded these values as less important compared to their younger counterparts. Our results about older Singaporeans contrasted with findings from research on LOV of older persons in other parts of the world, some of which examined both

Table 5.4 Correlations of LOV with age, gender, education, income and marital status (2016)

LOV	Age	Gender	Education	Household income	Marital status[1]
Sense of belonging	**-0.106** (*p*<.000)	0.036 (*p*<.162)	**0.093** (*p*<.000)	-0.009 (*p*<.732)	-0.028 (*p*<.293)
Security	**-0.097** (*p*<.000)	**0.076** (*p*<.000)	**0.108** (*p*<.000)	**-0.059** (*p*<.023)	-0.013 (*p*<.628)
Self-respect	**-0.190** (*p*<.000)	0.043 (*p*<.094)	**0.149** (*p*<.000)	-0.037 (*p*<.147)	**-0.111** (*p*<.000)
Warm relationships with others	**-0.168** (*p*<.000)	0.039 (*p*<.134)	**0.095** (*p*<.000)	-0.012 (*p*<.645)	**-0.078** (*p*<.004)
Fun and enjoyment	**-0.239** (*p*<.000)	-0.039 (*p*<.133)	**0.106** (*p*<.000)	-0.022 (*p*<.404)	**-0.116** (*p*<.000)
Being well-respected	**-0.189** (*p*<.000)	0.043 (*p*<.096)	0.050 (*p*<.051)	**0.064** (*p*<.014)	**-0.107** (*p*<.000)
Sense of accomplishment	**-0.297** (*p*<.000)	-0.050 (*p*<.051)	**0.170** (*p*<.000)	0.017 (*p*<.517)	**-0.150** (*p*<.000)
Self-fulfillment	**-0.251** (*p*<.000)	-0.011 (*p*<.660)	**0.213** (*p*<.000)	0.007 (*p*<.799)	**-0.159** (*p*<.000)
Excitement	**-0.417** (*p*<.000)	**-0.079** (*p*<.002)	**0.138** (*p*<.000)	-0.014 (*p*<.577)	**-0.262** (*p*<.000)

1 Includes only those who declared themselves as married or single.

Bold figures indicate significant correlations.

chronological age as well as cognitive or self-perceived age. For instance, in a study involving 356 Australian seniors ranging in age between 56 and 93 years, Cleaver and Muller (2002) found that those who had younger self-perceived age placed more importance on Fun and Enjoyment, while those who had older self-perceived age placed greater importance on Security.

In a study involving 650 older consumers (above 50 years of age) in the United Kingdom, Sudbury and Simcock (2009) found that the most important value to older consumers was Self-respect, followed by Security, Warm Relationships with Others, and a Sense of Accomplishment, with Being Well-respected the least important value. However, in terms of self-reported cognitive age, Sudbury and Simcock (2009) found that while Self-respect is of greatest importance to the older cognitive age groups (40s, 50s and 60s), the youngest cognitive age group (30s) placed the greatest importance on Warm Relationships with Others. Strong negative correlations were found between cognitive age and Warm Relationships with Others, Fun and Enjoyment, and Self-fulfillment. Strong positive correlations were found between cognitive age and Security, Sense of Accomplishment, and Sense of Belonging.

Gender

As far as Sense of Belonging, Warm Relationships with Others, Fun and Enjoyment, and Self-fulfillment are concerned, there were no gender differences (see Table 5.4 third column). However, female Singaporeans tended to hold values such as Security, Self-respect and Being Well-respected as more important than male Singaporeans, whereas male Singaporeans placed more emphasis on values like Sense of Accomplishment and Excitement. We have not found any extant studies that examined gender differences in LOV.

Education

Education had an unanimous positive and significant correlation with all nine values in LOV (see fourth column in Table 5.4), implying that as Singaporeans became more educated, they placed more importance on these nine values. We have not found any extant studies that examined differences between LOV and education.

Income

Household income had a negative and significant relationship with Security (see fifth column in Table 5.4) implying that Singaporeans tended to place less importance on Security as their income increased. However, income had a positive and significant relationship with Being Well-respected, implying that Singaporeans tended to value Being Well-respected more as their income increased. We have not found any extant studies that examined differences in LOV for income.

Marital Status

Marital status had a negative and significant relationship with Self-respect, Warm Relationships with Others, Fun and Enjoyment, Being Well-respected, Sense of Accomplishment, Self-fulfillment and Excitement (see sixth column in Table 5.4). This means that singles were significantly better off than married Singaporeans in these areas. We have not found any extant studies that examined differences in LOV for marital status.

Impact of LOV on subjective wellbeing

To assess the impact of LOV on Singaporeans' subjective wellbeing, we conducted a series of regression analyses, using the nine LOV items as independent variables. The subjective wellbeing indicators selected as dependent variables in the regression analyses are happiness ("All things considered, would you say that you are happy these days?" on a 5-point scale of "1 = very unhappy" to "5 = very happy"), enjoyment ("How often do you feel you are really enjoying life these days?" on a 4-point response scale of "1 = never" to "4 = often"), achievement ("How much do you feel you are accomplishing what you want out of life?" on a 4-point scale of "1 = none" to "4 = a great deal"), level of control ("How much control do you feel you have over important aspects of your life?" on a 4-point scale of "1 = none" to "4 = a great deal"), sense of purpose ("All things considered, how much do you feel you have a sense of purpose in your life?" on a 4-point scale of "1 = none" to "4 = a great deal"), satisfaction with life (factor scores for responses to five statements: "In most ways, my life is close to my ideal," "The conditions of my life are excellent," "I am satisfied with my life," "So far I have gotten the important things I want in life" and "If I could live my life over, I would change almost nothing" on a 6-point scale "1 = strongly disagree" to "6 = strongly agree"), satisfaction with overall quality of life ("Your overall quality of life" on a scale of "1 = very dissatisfied," "2 = dissatisfied," "3 = somewhat dissatisfied," 4 for "somewhat satisfied," "5 = satisfied" and "6 = very satisfied") and satisfaction with overall quality of life in Singapore (on a scale of "1 = very dissatisfied," "2 = dissatisfied," "3 = somewhat dissatisfied," "4 = somewhat satisfied," "5 = satisfied" and "6 = very satisfied").

LOV and happiness

As shown in the second column of Table 5.5, out of the nine values, only Sense of Belonging had a positive and significant impact on Singaporeans' happiness.

LOV and enjoyment

Sense of Belonging, Self-respect, and Fun and Enjoyment were the three LOV items that had a positive and significant impact on Singaporeans' enjoyment level, while Being Well-respected had a negative and significant impact, as shown in the third column of Table 5.5.

LOV and achievement

Table 5.5 (fourth column) shows that Sense of Belonging, Fun and Enjoyment, and Self-fulfillment had a positive and significant impact on Singaporeans' sense of achievement, while Excitement exerted a negative and significant impact.

LOV and control

For a sense of control over important aspects of Singaporeans' life, Security, Fun and Enjoyment, and Self-fulfillment played positive and significant roles, as shown in the fifth column of Table 5.5, while Excitement significantly took away something from this impact.

LOV and purpose

As shown in the sixth column six of Table 5.5, Sense of Belonging and Self-Fulfillment contributed positively and significantly toward Singaporeans' sense of purpose in life, but Being Well-respected had a negative significant impact.

Table 5.5 Impact of LOV on happiness, enjoyment, achievement, control and purpose

LOV items	Unstandardized beta				
	Happiness[1]	Enjoyment[2]	Achievement[3]	Control[4]	Purpose[5]
Constant	**2.186**	**1.680**	**1.730**	**1.494**	**1.433**
	(p<.000)	**(p<.000)**	**(p<.000)**	**(p<.000)**	**(p<.000)**
Sense of belonging	**0.151**	**0.064**	**0.103**	0.043	**0.121**
	(p<.000)	**(p<.050)**	**(p<.000)**	(p<.144)	**(p<.000)**
Security	−0.030	0.012	0.040	**0.081**	0.060
	(p<.512)	(p<.745)	(p<.225)	**(p<.012)**	(p<.070)
Self-respect	0.028	**0.119**	0.026	0.032	0.062
	(p<.561)	**(p<.002)**	(p<.447)	(p<.348)	(p<.075)
Warm relationships with others	0.082	0.000	−0.009	0.023	0.026
	(p<.071)	(p<.989)	(p<.791)	(p<.478)	(p<.426)
Fun and enjoyment	0.037	**0.093**	**0.053**	**0.074**	0.048
	(p<.284)	**(p<.001)**	**(p<.031)**	**(p<.003)**	(p<.055)
Being well-respected	0.036	**−0.068**	−0.001	0.001	**−0.057**
	(p<.309)	**(p<.015)**	(p<.955)	(p<.968)	**(p<.025)**
Sense of accomplishment	−0.030	−0.007	−0.005	−0.013	0.018
	(p<.472)	(p<.821)	(p<.877)	(p<.659)	(p<.552)
Self-fulfillment	0.018	0.065	**0.075**	**0.081**	**0.066**
	(p<.678)	(p<.064)	**(p<.017)**	**(p<.009)**	**(p<.039)**
Excitement	−0.006	−0.018	**−0.058**	**−0.032**	−0.028
	(p<.788)	(p<.318)	**(p<.000)**	**(p<.042)**	(p<.083)

1. $R^2 = 0.038$; F-value = 6.585, p<.000.
2. $R^2 = 0.052$; F-value = 9.069, p<.000.
3. $R^2 = 0.050$; F-value = 8.779, p<.000.
4. $R^2 = 0.063$; F-value = 11.162, p<.000.
5. $R^2 = 0.078$; F-value = 14.044, p<.000.

Bold figures indicate statistical significance.

LOV and satisfaction with life

Having a Sense of Belonging, Warm Relationships with Others, and Being Well-respected had a positive and significant impact on Singaporeans' satisfaction with life, but Sense of Accomplishment had a significantly negative impact, as shown in Table 5.6 (second column).

LOV and satisfaction with overall quality of life

Sense of Belonging, Warm Relationships with Others, and Fun and Enjoyment had a positive and significant impact on Singaporeans' satisfaction with their overall quality of life, as shown in Table 5.6 (third column).

Table 5.6 Impact of LOV on satisfaction with life, satisfaction with overall quality of life and satisfaction with overall quality of life in Singapore

LOV items	Unstandardized beta		
	Satisfaction with life[1]	Satisfaction with overall quality of life[2]	Satisfaction with overall quality of life in Singapore[3]
(Constant)	**2.576** **(*p*<.000)**	**2.860** **(*p*<.000)**	**2.777** **(*p*<.000)**
Sense of belonging	**0.160** **(*p*<.000)**	**0.129** **(*p*<.000)**	**0.118** **(*p*<.001)**
Security	0.007 (*p*<.871)	0.038 (*p*<.314)	**0.081** **(*p*<.040)**
Self-respect	−0.015 (*p*<.748)	0.004 (*p*<.926)	0.041 (*p*<.327)
Warm relationships with others	**0.086** **(*p*<.046)**	**0.098** **(*p*<.008)**	**0.089** **(*p*<.022)**
Fun and enjoyment	0.060 (*p*<.065)	**0.085** **(*p*<.003)**	0.004 (*p*<.899)
Being well-respected	**0.110** **(*p*<.001)**	0.044 (*p*<.129)	**0.086** **(*p*<.005)**
Sense of accomplishment	**−0.113** **(*p*<.004)**	−0.030 (*p*<.379)	−0.010 (*p*<.784)
Self-fulfillment	0.061 (*p*<.145)	0.028 (*p*<.437)	−0.018 (*p*<.642)
Excitement	−0.011 (*p*<.592)	−0.024 (*p*<.184)	−0.019 (*p*<.321)

1. $R^2 = 0.063$; *F*-value = 11.127, *p*<.000.
2. $R^2 = 0.079$; *F*-value = 14.292, *p*<.000.
3. $R^2 = 0.075$; *F*-value = 13.456, *p*<.000.

Bold figures indicate statistical significance.

LOV and satisfaction with overall quality of life in Singapore

Finally, Sense of Belonging, Security, Warm Relationships with Others, and Being Well-respected had a positive and significant impact on Singaporeans' satisfaction with overall quality of life in Singapore, as shown in Table 5.6 (fourth column).

Schwartz's Portrait Values Questionnaire (PVQ)

For the 2016 QOL Survey, we provided Singaporeans with 21 descriptions of different individuals and asked the respondents to indicate to what extent they are like the persons described ("1 = not like me at all" to "6 = very much like me"). These 21 statements were from the Portrait Values Questionnaire (PVQ), which is a shorter version of the original Schwartz Values Survey (SVS) that had 56 or

57 items (Schwartz 2012). The PVQ was used in the European Social Survey (ESS) to measure basic human values in 20 countries in Europe (Schwartz 2007). Each of the 21 statements was indexed to ten basic values identified by Schwartz (2007) as Self-direction, Stimulation, Hedonism, Achievement, Power, Security, Conformity, Tradition, Benevolence and Universalism. The basic value of Self-direction was measured by one statement relating to being creative and doing things in his or her own ways and by another statement relating to being free and being independent. Stimulation was measured by one statement relating to seeking and doing new/different things in life and by another statement relating to being adventurous and risk seeking. Hedonism was measured by two statements relating to self-indulgence in fun and pleasure. Achievement was measured by two statements relating to showing abilities and being admired and being successful and recognized for his or her achievement. Power was measured by two statements relating to having wealth and authority. Security was measured by two statements relating to living in a secure and safe environment and national security. Conformity was measured by two statements relating to being obedient and exercising self-discipline. Tradition was measured by two statements relating to respect for tradition, and being humble and modest. Benevolence was measured by two statements relating to being helpful and loyal. And Universalism was measured by three statements relating to being broadminded, believing in equality and caring for nature.

A factor analysis of the 21 statements showed that there were four factors (known as Higher Order Values) with the following dimensions: Openness (or Openness to change), Conservation, Self-transcendence and Self-enhancement (Schwartz 2007). The Openness dimension includes the basic values of Stimulation, Self-direction, and Hedonism. The Conservation dimension includes the basic values of Conformity, Tradition and Security. The Self-transcendence dimension includes the basic values of universalism and benevolence. The Self-enhancement dimension includes the basic values of Achievement and Power.

Table 5.7 shows the factor analysis results for the four Higher Order Values for the 2016 QOL Survey compared to results for the ESS as reported in Schwartz (2007). As shown in Table 5.7, the reliability ratios (Cronbach alphas)

Table 5.7 Cronbach alpha reliabilities, means and standard deviations of the four Higher Order Values for the 2016 QOL Survey and the European Social Survey

Schwartz's higher order values	Number of items		Cronbach alpha		Importance mean (based on Ipsatized scores)		Importance standard deviation	
	ESS (2007)	2016 QOL Survey	ESS (2007)	2016 QOL Survey	ESS (2007)	2016 QOL Survey	ESS (2007)	2016 QOL Survey
Openness	6	6	0.75	0.78	−0.14	−0.26	0.64	0.50
Conservation	6	6	0.73	0.76	0.09	0.30	0.69	0.50
Self-transcendence	5	5	0.69	0.78	0.52	0.46	0.45	0.43
Self-enhancement	4	4	0.72	0.74	−0.68	−0.63	0.74	0.60

for the Higher Order Values of the Singapore sample (2016 QOL Survey) were higher than those for the ESS sample.

Value priorities

The importance means for the 2016 QOL sample are in line with the ESS sample, as shown in Table 5.7. The means for the ESS sample show that the European countries gave high priority to Self-transcendence and low priority to Self-enhancement (Schwartz 2007). Singaporeans also gave higher priority to Self-transcendence and to Conservation, which the Europeans gave lower priority to (Schwartz 2007). Unlike the Europeans, Singaporeans gave even lower priority to Openness (–0.26 versus –0.14), although Singaporeans gave almost as low a priority to Self-enhancement as the Europeans (–0.63 versus –0.68).

Sources of individual differences in Higher Order Values

Age

Researchers have posited that, as people age, "they tend to become more embedded in social networks, more committed to habitual patterns, and less exposed to arousing and exciting changes and challenges" (Glen 1974; Tyler and Schuler 1991). Thus it was implied that Conservation values should increase with age, while Openness should decrease (Schwartz 2007). This was supported by Doran and Littrell's (2013) online survey of 440 White, non-Hispanic American adults, which found that older subjects reported significantly lower means for Stimulation and Hedonism (values in the Openness factor).

Researchers also found that once people started having families of their own and achieving good positions in their careers, "they tend to become less preoccupied with their own strivings and more concerned with the welfare of others" (Veroff et al. 1984). Thus it was implied that Self-transcendence values should increase with age and Self-enhancement values should decrease (Schwartz 2007). The 20 European countries in the ESS showed that "all the observed correlations confirm the expected associations and support the probable processes of influence" (Schwartz 2007, p. 180). This was also supported in the American sample in Doran and Littrell (2013). They found that older participants had significantly lower means for achievement (a value in the Self-enhancement factor).

As shown in Table 5.8, age was negatively correlated with Openness and Self-enhancement and positively correlated with Conservation for Singaporeans, similar to the ESS sample. However, unlike the Europeans, age was negatively correlated with Self-transcendence.

Gender

Although many theories of gender differences led researchers to postulate that "men emphasize 'agentic-instrumental' values such as power and achievement, while females emphasize 'expressive-communal' values such as benevolence and universalism" (Schwartz and Rubel 2005), most theories expect the differences to be small (Schwartz 2007). In the ESS, Schwartz (2007) found this expectation held true for gender. Doran and Littrell (2013) found that females had significantly higher-value means for universalism and benevolence (the Self-transcendence factor) and males had significantly higher means for Self-direction and Stimulation (the Openness factor) and Achievement and Power (the Self-enhancement factor).

In Singapore, the gender effect was not significant for the values of Self-transcendence and Conservation (see Table 5.8), while Openness and Self-enhancement were negatively correlated with gender (meaning that males emphasized these values more than females). Although Conservation had a positive relationship with gender in Singapore (meaning that females placed more emphasis on this value than males), the relationship was not statistically significant.

Education

Although educational experiences can increase openness to nonroutine ideas and activities central to Stimulation values, they can challenge an unquestioning acceptance of prevailing norms, expectations, and traditions, thereby undermining Conformity and Tradition. The increasing competencies to cope with life that people acquire through education may also reduce the importance of Security values (Schwartz 2007). The ESS showed a positive relationship between years of education and Openness values and a negative association with Conservation values (Schwartz 2007). Additionally, Schwartz (2007) found that "education was positively associated with achievement values," while this linear relationship did not apply to Universalism. The positive correlation applied only to postsecondary education and was substantially higher for university educated people. In America, Doran and Littrell (2013) found that the more highly educated subjects in their study had significantly lower means for Conformity, Tradition, Security (values in the Conservation factor) and Hedonism (a value in the Openness factor). As shown in Table 5.8, education was positively correlated with Openness, Self-enhancement and Self-transcendence in Singapore, similar to what was found for the European countries. Although Conservation had a negative relationship with education in Singapore, this relationship was not statistically significant.

Income

According to Schwartz (2007), higher income was expected to promote the prioritization of the Stimulation, Self-direction, Hedonism and Achievement values over the Security, Conformity and Tradition values. In his analysis of the 20 countries in the ESS, Schwartz (2007) found that income contributed to higher Stimulation, Hedonism and Self-direction (Openness factor) and to Achievement and Power (Self-enhancement factor). In America, Doran and

Table 5.8 Correlations of the four Higher Order Values with age, gender, education, income and marital status (2016)

Higher order value	Age	Gender	Education	Household income	Marital status[1]
Openness	**−0.392** (*p*<**.000**)	**−0.123** (*p*<**.000**)	**0.181** (*p*<**.000**)	**0.085** (*p*<**.000**)	**−0.223** (*p*<**.000**)
Self-enhancement	**−0.282** (*p*<**.000**)	**−0.156** (*p*<**.000**)	**0.123** (*p*<**.000**)	**0.152** (*p*<**.000**)	**−0.121** (*p*<**.000**)
Self-transcendence	**−0.116** (*p*<**.000**)	0.011 (*p*<.659)	**0.086** (*p*<**.001**)	**0.067** (*p*<**.010**)	**−0.113** (*p*<**.000**)
Conservation	**0.067** (*p*<**.009**)	0.044 (*p*<.086)	−0.020 (*p*<.431)	0.049 (*p*<.060)	**0.082** (*p*<**.002**)

1 Includes only those who declared themselves as married or single.

Bold figures indicate significant correlations.

Littrell (2013) found that higher-income subjects in their study had significantly higher-value means for Power (Self-enhancement factor) and Security (Conservation factor) but significantly lower means for Universalism (Self-transcendence factor).

Similar to the case of the European countries, income had a positive relationship with Openness in Singapore (see Table 5.8). Like the European countries and America, income had a positive relationship with Self-enhancement in Singapore. However, unlike the case of Europe and America, income had a positive relationship with Self-transcendence, and as in the case of America, income had a positive relationship with Conservation in Singapore, although the relationship was not statistically significant.

Marital status

In the case of Singapore, marital status had a negative and significant relationship with Openness, Self-enhancement and Self-transcendence (see sixth column of Table 5.8). However, marital status had a positive and significant relationship with Conservatism. This means that married people placed less emphasis on Openness, Self-enhancement, and Self-transcendence but more emphasis on Conservatism compared to the singles. Note that we have not found any extant studies that examined the relationship between the Higher Order Values and marital status.

Impact of Schwartz's Higher Order Values on subjective wellbeing

To assess the impact of Schwartz's Higher Order Values on Singaporeans' subjective wellbeing, we conducted a series of regression analyses, using the factor scores for the four factors forming the four Higher Order Values as independent variables. The subjective wellbeing indicators selected as dependent variables in the regression analyses are the same as those for the Personal Values analyses: happiness, enjoyment, accomplishment, control, purpose, satisfaction with life, satisfaction with overall quality of life and satisfaction with overall quality of life in Singapore.

Impact of Higher Order Values on happiness, enjoyment, achievement, control and purpose

As shown in the second column of Table 5.9, of the four Higher Order Values, only Conservation had a positive and significant impact on Singaporeans' Happiness. Openness and Conservation had a positive and significant impact on Singaporeans' Enjoyment, while Self-enhancement had a negative and significant impact (Table 5.9, third column). Conservation had a positive and significant impact on Singaporeans' Achievement (see Table 5.9, fourth column).

Self-transcendence and Conservation had a significant and positive impact on Control (see Table 5.9, fifth column), while only Self-transcendence had a positive and significant impact on Purpose (see Table 5.9, sixth column).

Table 5.9 Higher Order Values and happiness, enjoyment, achievement, control and purpose

Higher order values	Unstandardized beta				
	Happiness[1]	Enjoyment[2]	Achievement[3]	Control[4]	Purpose[5]
(Constant)	3.607 ($p<.000$)	3.002 ($p<.000$)	2.897 ($p<.000$)	2.971 ($p<.000$)	3.040 ($p<.000$)
Openness	0.032 ($p<.298$)	**0.049** ($p<.048$)	−0.014 ($p<.512$)	0.004 ($p<.851$)	0.009 ($p<.685$)
Self-enhancement	−0.003 ($p<.920$)	**−0.072** ($p<.002$)	−0.021 ($p<.313$)	−0.022 ($p<.301$)	−0.031 ($p<.153$)
Self-transcendence	−0.004 ($p<.893$)	0.034 ($p<.188$)	0.026 ($p<.252$)	**0.045** ($p<.047$)	**0.081** ($p<.001$)
Conservation	**0.093** ($p<.002$)	**0.051** ($p<.036$)	**0.078** ($p<.000$)	**0.053** ($p<.016$)	0.029 ($p<.190$)

1. R^2 = 0.014; *F*-value = 5.403, $p<.000$.
2. R^2 = 0.016; *F*-value = 6.127, $p<.000$.
3. R^2 = 0.089; *F*-value = 9.122, $p<.000$.
4. R^2 = 0.019; *F*-value = 7.059, $p<.000$.
5. R^2 = 0.024; *F*-value = 9.106, $p<.000$.

Bold figures indicate statistical significance.

Impact of Higher Order Values on satisfaction
with life, satisfaction with overall quality of life and
satisfaction with overall quality of life in Singapore

For satisfaction with life, only Conservation had a positive and significant impact (see Table 5.10 second column). For satisfaction with overall quality of life, Self-transcendence and Conservation had a positive and significant impact (see Table 5.10, third column). Finally, for satisfaction with overall quality of life in Singapore, Openness had a negative and significant impact, while Self-transcendence and Conservation had a positive and significant impact (see Table 5.10 fourth column).

Conclusion

Our investigation of Singaporeans' ranking of the importance of the nine values in the LOV showed that there were no significant shifts in value importance over the past two decades (1996 to 2016) compared to what was found in America (e.g., Gurel-Atay et al.'s (2010) study of Americans for the period 1976 to 2007). In terms of top-ranked and lowest-ranked values, it was interesting to note that, unlike their Western counterparts, Singaporeans had consistently placed lowest importance on values like Fun and Enjoyment, and Excitement. The lack of emphasis on these values seemed to reflect the Confucian nature

Table 5.10 Higher Order Values and satisfaction with life, satisfaction with overall quality of life and satisfaction with overall quality of life in Singapore

Higher order values	*Unstandardized Beta*		
	Satisfaction with life[1]	*Satisfaction with overall quality of life*[2]	*Satisfaction with overall quality of life in Singapore*[3]
(Constant)	**4.287** **(*p*<.000)**	**4.725** **(*p*<.000)**	**4.657** **(*p*<.000)**
Openness	0.026 (*p*<.361)	0.027 (*p*<.296)	**−0.074** **(*p*<.006)**
Self-enhancement	0.002 (*p*<.932)	−0.035 (*p*<.151)	0.005 (*p*<.856)
Self-transcendence	−0.005 (*p*<.879)	**0.056** **(*p*<.035)**	**0.075** **(*p*<.007)**
Conservation	**0.222** **(*p*<.000)**	**0.102** **(*p*<.000)**	**0.087** **(*p*<.001)**

1. R^2 = 0.706, *F*-value = 31.014, *p*<.000.
2. R^2 = 0.039, *F*-value = 15.332, *p*<.000.
3. R^2 = 0.031, *F*-value = 12.039, *p*<.000.

Bold figures indicate statistical significance.

of Singaporean society where diligence takes precedence over play in work attitudes. Singapore is one of the societies belonging geographically to "Confucian Asia," a region infused with the norms and values taught by Confucius and Mencius (Slingerland 2003).

In 2016, age and education were the most important sources of individual differences across all nine values in LOV (Sense of Belonging, Security, Self-respect, Warm Relationships with Others, Fun and Enjoyment, Being Well-respected, Sense of Accomplishment, Self-fulfillment, and Excitement), followed closely by marital status, which had differential impacts on seven values (Self-respect, Warm Relationships with Others, Fun and Enjoyment, Being Well-respected, Sense of Accomplishment, Self-fulfillment, Excitement). Household incomes had the least impact, only contributing to individual differences on the value of Security.

We have shown that older Singaporeans (in terms of chronological age) did not share the same value importance as their younger counterparts. It would be interesting if we had also examined cognitive or self-perceived age besides chronological age because some of the research in the West has shown that using cognitive age could provide valuable insights (Sudbury and Simcock 2009). More insights could be drawn if there were cross-country studies that would allow us to make comparisons with our findings on the significant demographic differences.

In 2016, different values of LOV have differential effects on Singaporeans' subjective wellbeing. Sense of Belonging, Fun and Enjoyment, and Self-fulfillment were three values that had the most significant influence on Singaporeans' subjective wellbeing. Sense of Belonging had a positive influence on Singaporeans' Happiness, Enjoyment, Achievement and Purpose, while Fun and Enjoyment and Self-fulfillment both had a positive influence on Enjoyment, Achievement, Control and Purpose. It is interesting to note that the next most important value of Excitement was also a value that had a negative impact on Singaporeans' Achievement, Control and Purpose. Warm Relationships with Others and Sense of Accomplishment had no impact at all on Singaporeans' Happiness, Enjoyment, Achievement, Control and Purpose. The absence of any significant impact on happiness of values such as Fun and Enjoyment and Excitement is in line with what Shin and Inoguchi (2009) found in a survey of seven Confucian societies, including Singapore, that feelings of enjoyment alone do not lead to a happy life among the vast majority of the people living in these societies, but only when these people experience enjoyment together with achievement of goals and/or the satisfaction of desires and needs would they be happy or very happy with their lives.

When examining the impact of LOV on subjective wellbeing in terms of life satisfaction, Sense of Belonging, and Warm Relationships with Others were the two most important values that had a positive influence on Singaporeans' satisfaction with life, satisfaction with overall quality of life, and satisfaction with overall quality of life in Singapore. Security positively influenced only Singaporeans' satisfaction with overall quality of life in Singapore, while Sense of

Accomplishment positively influenced only Singaporeans' satisfaction with life. The values of Self-respect, Self-fulfillment, and Excitement had no significant roles to play on Singaporeans' life satisfaction.

We used Schwartz's PVQ for the first time in our 2016 QOL Survey and found that the 21 values from Schwartz's PVQ fitted well into the four Higher Order Values of Openness, Conservation, Self-transcendence, and Self-enhancement, with better reliability than the ESS for 20 European countries (Schwartz 2007).

Europeans and Singaporeans were alike in terms of according high priority to Self-transcendence and low priority to Self-enhancement. However, unlike the Europeans, Singaporeans gave high priority to Conservation and Openness. Perhaps more cross-country and cross-cultural studies could be done to develop more insights into these similarities and differences.

In 2016, demographics contributed as sources of individual differences in all four Higher Order Values, with the exceptions of gender and education for two of the values. Gender had a positive but not significant correlation with Self-transcendence in Singapore, unlike the case of Europe and America. Education had a negative but not significant correlation with Conservation for Singaporeans, unlike America where higher education was linked with the lower importance placed on Conservation.

The four Higher Order Values had differential effects on Singaporeans' subjective wellbeing. Conservation had the most wide-ranging impact on seven out of eight wellbeing indicators, followed by Self-transcendence for four wellbeing indicators (including Control and Purpose). Understandably, Self-enhancement and Openness had an impact on enjoyment. In noting these effects, we also observed some convergence with the effects of the LOV on subjective wellbeing for the wellbeing indicators of Enjoyment and Control and, to a lesser extent, on satisfaction with the overall quality of life and satisfaction with the quality of life in Singapore.

Conservation was the only Higher Order Value that had an influence (positive) on Singaporeans' happiness. Openness and Conservation contributed positively toward Singaporeans' Enjoyment, but Self-enhancement had a negative impact. The Higher Order Value of Openness included values of Stimulation and Hedonism, and their positive impact on Enjoyment was also in line with our findings that Fun and Enjoyment (from the LOV) had a positive and significant impact on Enjoyment. The Higher Order Value of Self-enhancement included the value of Achievement and Power, and their negative impact on Singaporeans' Enjoyment was in line with our findings that Being Well-respected and Sense of Accomplishment (from the LOV) had a negative impact on Enjoyment (although it was not significant for Sense of Accomplishment). Conservation was the only higher order value to have an influence (positive) on Singaporeans' Achievement.

Conservation and Self-transcendence were two Higher Order Values that had an influence (positive) on Singaporeans' control over important aspects of their life. This finding about the Security component in Conservation corresponded to what we found about Security (from the LOV) having a positive influence on Singaporeans' control over life's important events. The only Higher Order Value that had an influence (positive) on Singaporeans' sense of purpose in life was Self-transcendence, which included values of universalism and benevolence.

Conservation was the only Higher Order Value having an influence (positive) over Singaporeans' satisfaction with life. Self-transcendence and Conservation were two Higher Order Values influencing (positively) Singaporeans' satisfaction with overall quality of life and Singaporeans' satisfaction with overall quality of life in Singapore, although Openness had a negative influence only on satisfaction with overall quality of life in Singapore. Given that Self-transcendence included the value of Benevolence, these findings corresponded partially to our finding on LOV that maintaining Warm Relationships with Others, among other values, had a positive and significant impact on Singaporeans' satisfaction with their overall quality of life, as well as satisfaction with overall quality of life in Singapore.

In conclusion, values, whether in terms of the nine-item List of Values or the four-dimensional Schwartz's Higher Order Values, have a significant influence on Singaporeans' subjective wellbeing. Our findings also showed that certain values in LOV could be mapped to some of the basic values in Schwartz's PVQ (Schwartz 2007). Taken together, these two value systems provided a more holistic picture of the relationship between values and subjective wellbeing in Singapore.

References

Cleaver, M., and Muller, T.E. (2002), 'I want to pretend I'm eleven years younger: Subjective age and seniors' motives for vacation travel', *Social Indicators Research*, 60, 227–241.

Doran, C.J., and Littrell, R.F. (2013), 'Measuring mainstream US cultural values', *Journal of Business Ethics*, 117, 261–280.

Glen, N.D. (1974), 'Aging and conservatism', *Annuals of the American Academy of Political and Social Science*, 415, 176–186.

Grunert, S.C., and Scherhorn, G. (1990), 'Consumer values in West Germany underlying dimensions and cross-cultural comparison with North America', *Journal of Business Research*, 20, 97–107.

Gurel-Atay, E., Xie, G.X., Chen, J., and Kahle, L.R. (2010), 'Changes in social values in the United States, 1976–2007', *Journal of Advertising Research*, 50(1), 57–67.

Kahle, L.R. (1983), *Social values and social change: Adaptation to life in America*, New York, NY, USA: Praeger.

Kahle, L.R. (1996), 'Social values and consumer behavior: Research from the list of values', in *The psychology of values: The Ontario symposium*, edited by C. Seligman, J.M. Olson and M.P Zanna, Vol. 8, Mahwah, NJ, USA: Lawrence Erlbaum.

Kau, A.K., Jung, K., Tambyah, S.K., and Tan, S.J. (2004), *Understanding Singaporeans: Values, lifestyles, aspirations, and consumption behaviors*, Singapore: World Scientific Publishing.

Kau, A.K., Tan, S.J., and Wirtz, J. (1998), *Seven faces of Singaporeans: Their values, aspirations and lifestyles*, Singapore: Prentice Hall.

Mitchell, A. (1983), *The nine American lifestyles*, New York, NY, USA: Macmillan.

Rokeach, M. (1968), *Beliefs, attitudes, values*, San Francisco, CA, USA: Jossey-Bass.

Rokeach, M. (1973), *The nature of human values*, New York, NY, USA: Free Press.

Schwartz, S.H. (2007), 'Value orientations: Measurement, antecedents and consequences across nations', in *Measuring attitudes cross-nationally: Lessons from the European Social Survey*, edited by R. Jowell, C. Roberts, R. Fitzgerald and G. Eva, London, UK: Sage, 169–203.

Schwartz, S.H. (2012), 'An overview of the Schwartz theory of basic values', *Online Readings in Psychology and Culture*, 2(1). http://dx.doi.org/10.9707/2307-0919.1116.

Schwartz, S.H., and Rubel, T. (2005), 'Sex differences in value priorities: Cross-cultural and multi-method studies', *Journal of Personality and Social Psychology*, 89, 1010–1028.

Shin, D.D., and Inoguchi, I. (2009), 'Avowed happiness in Confucian Asia: Ascertaining its distribution, patterns, and sources,' *Social Indicators Research*, 92, 405–427.

Slingerland, E. (2003), *Confucius analects*, Indianapolis, IN, USA: Hackett Publishing.

Stockard, J., Carpenter, C., and Kahle, L. (2014), 'Continuity and change in values in midlife: Testing the age stability hypothesis', *Experimental Aging Research*, 40(2), 224–244.

Sudbury, L., and Simcock, P. (2009), 'Understanding older consumers through cognitive age and the list of values: A U.K.-based perspective', *Psychology and Marketing*, 20(1), 22–38.

Tambyah, S.K., and Tan, S.J. (2013), *Happiness and wellbeing: The Singaporean experience*, London, UK: Routledge.

Tyler, T.R., and Schuler, R.A. (1991), 'Aging and attitude change', *Journal of Personality and Social Psychology*, 61, 689–697.

Veroff, J., Reuman, D., and Feld, S. (1984), 'Motives in American men and women across the adult life span', *Developmental Psychology*, 20, 1142–1158.

World Values Survey. www.worldvaluessurvey.org/WVSContents.jsp (accessed November 17, 2017).

6 Clustering of Singaporeans

In this chapter, we continue our inquiry into the influence of values on subjective wellbeing. We examine value orientations on a broader scale by using them to distinguish among clusters of Singaporeans. The value orientations cover both traditional and modern attitudes specific to the Singapore context. These value orientations had been used for the clustering of Singaporeans in two prior surveys (the 2001 Survey and the 2011 QOL Survey). Some value orientations are more pro-social and other-oriented, while some are more self-centered. For the 2016 QOL Survey, respondents were asked for their views on 31 statements on various value orientations. These include family values, eco-orientation, status consciousness, volunteerism, traditionalism, entrepreneurial spirit, and materialism. All items used to measure value orientations in the 2011 QOL survey were retained, except for one of the three statements on materialism ("Money is the most important thing to consider in choosing a job") and six statements on e-orientation. These statements were dropped based on a review of the relevance and currency of the value orientations being measured. The responses ranged from "1 = strongly disagree" to "6 = strongly agree." Higher means thus indicated greater agreement about a particular statement.

Identification of factors

Principal component factor analysis was conducted to derive the respective underlying dimensions of Singaporeans' value orientations. An initial principal component factor analysis of the 31 statements on Value Orientations yielded seven factors that had eigen values above 1 and that explained 62.83 percent of the variance, with all items loaded above 0.5 (Nunnally 1978). The seven factors, the statements measuring the value orientations, their loadings and reliability alphas are indicated in Table 6.1. These factors and value orientations were then used to organize Singaporeans into the distinctive clusters.

- *Family Values (Factor 1):* This factor has seven statements that are similar to the Family Values factor derived in the 2001 Survey and the 2011 QOL Survey. The factor explained 19.74 percent of the total variance.

- *Eco-orientation (Factor 2):* This factor has the same five statements in the factor named as Eco-orientation in the 2011 QOL Survey. This factor was named Eco-orientation because the statements referred to environmentally responsible behaviors and choices. This factor explained 11.49 percent of the total variance.

- *Status Consciousness (Factor 3):* This factor has six statements all relating to status consciousness, unlike the factor in the 2011 QOL Survey, which combined all the five items in the Status Consciousness factor in the 2001 Survey and two out of the three items from the Materialism factor in the 2001 Survey. This factor explained 10.08 percent of the total variance.

- *Volunteerism (Factor 4):* This factor has four statements relating to volunteerism as opposed to three items in the 2011 QOL Survey. This factor explained 8.42 percent of the total variance.

- *Traditionalism (Factor 5):* This factor has all the five statements that made up the Traditionalism factor in the 2001 survey, unlike the 2011 QOL Survey when the factor included only three statements measuring respondents' attitudes about divorce, religion and premarital sex, which were not related to traditions and was named Conservatism then in 2011. We now name this factor Traditionalism. It explained 4.99 percent of the total variance.

- *Entrepreneurial Spirit (Factor 6):* This factor has the same three statements as the Entrepreneurial Spirit factor in the 2001 and 2011 surveys. It explained 4.24 percent of the total variance.

- *Materialism (Factor 7):* This factor contains the two statements relating to money ("Money can solve most people's problems" and "If I had to choose between having more money and leisure, I would choose more money"). This factor explained 3.87 percent of the total variance.

As described, three out of the seven factors in the 2016 QOL Survey are identical to their counterparts in 2011 and are measured by the same statements on value orientations. These three factors are Family Values, Eco-orientation and Entrepreneurial Spirit. Another three factors in 2016 retained some of the statements used for their counterparts in 2011. The Status Consciousness factor now includes all statements relating to status. The two statements relating to money in the Status Consciousness factor in the 2011 QOL Survey now form the Materialism factor in 2016. The factors Volunteerism and Traditionalism, with five and four statements respectively, have become more focused compared to the respective Volunteerism and Conservatism factors in 2011.

Generally, there was some stability in the value orientations being measured as the items within each value orientation remained about the same over the years (2016 compared to 2011 and 2001). The factor analyses and Cronbach alphas indicated a fairly robust and internally consistent structure for the various value orientations (see Table 6.1). In the sections to follow, we describe each factor and value orientation in detail. For each factor and value orientation, we

Table 6.1 Seven factors and factor loadings (2016)

Factors and value orientations	Factor loadings
Factor 1: Family values (19.74% variance explained; Cronbach alpha 0.898)	
One should support one's parents in their old age.	0.742
Family members should stand by one another through the ups and downs in life.	0.865
Family love makes a person feel appreciated and treasured.	0.820
One should honor one's parents and grandparents.	0.834
Family members should communicate openly and honestly with each other.	0.738
One should strive to provide the best for one's children.	0.742
Family members should be prepared to make sacrifices to help each other.	0.726
Factor 2: Eco-orientation (11.49% variance explained; Cronbach alpha 0.842)	
I am willing to pay more for products that are friendly to the environment.	0.874
I will stop buying my favourite brand if I know the company producing it was polluting the environment.	0.761
I usually buy products that use recyclable packaging.	0.771
I would be willing to bring my own bags for shopping to reduce the use of nonrecyclable bags.	0.758
I would be willing to use a nonpolluting detergent even if I have my laundry less white.	0.783
Factor 3: Status consciousness (10.08% variance explained; Cronbach alpha 0.868)	
I usually look out for well-known brands to reflect my status in life.	0.803
I like to own things that impress people.	0.869
I admire people who own expensive homes, cars and clothes.	0.784
I feel good if the credit card I use gives the impression of high status with exclusive privileges.	0.807
My social status is an important part of my life.	0.540
Factor 4: Volunteerism (8.42% variance explained; Cronbach alpha 0.832)	
I am willing to do volunteer work on a regular basis.	0.792
I often find time to be involved in community or charity work.	0.803
I feel I should do my part to help raise funds for charity.	0.760
I often donate money for charitable causes	0.695
Factor 5: Traditionalism (4.99% variance explained; Cronbach alpha 0.758)	
Divorce is unacceptable.	0.653
Religion is an important part of my life.	0.640
It is wrong to have sex before marriage.	0.755
I like to stick to traditional ways of doing things	0.801
I celebrate festivals in the traditional way.	0.686

Factors and value orientations	Factor loadings
Factor 6: Entrepreneurial spirit (4.24% variance explained; Cronbach alpha 0.643)	
I am creative and resourceful in solving problems.	0.783
I have more self-confidence than most people.	0.796
To me, realizing my fullest potential is more important than monetary rewards.	0.610
Factor 7: Materialism (3.87% variance explained; Cronbach alpha 0.758)	
Money can solve most people's problems.	0.817
If I had to choose between having more money and leisure, I would choose more money.	0.789

discuss the mean scores and how they compare with the 2001 Survey and the 2011 QOL Survey where applicable.

Family Values

The first factor is labeled Family Values. While a search of the literature did not reveal any studies that examined family values in detail, this value orientation is uniquely Singaporean. The Singapore Government has played a major role in promoting and upholding the importance of family values since 1994 through its Family Values campaign. The five shared family values that were purported to enhance the wellbeing of families and underpin the progress of Singapore were identified as (1) love, care and concern, (2) mutual respect, (3) filial responsibility, (4) commitment and (5) communication. We have used the same statements for the Family Values orientation for the 2001 and 2011 QOL Surveys. As shown in Table 6.2, the scores for all the seven statements measuring Family Values and the composite score have improved substantially in 2016 compared to 2011 and 2001. This was an encouraging result as it demonstrated that more than two decades after the Family Values campaign was started in 1994, Singaporeans were increasingly supportive of the core family values promoted. Singaporeans in 2016 gave top consideration to honoring one's grandparents and parents, which used to be ranked second in 2011 and fourth in 2001. The scores for Statements A, B and C (in Table 6.2) also highlighted the importance Singaporeans placed on caring for the elderly and family love.

Eco-orientation

The second factor containing statements measuring eco-orientation in the 2016 QOL Survey is shown in Table 6.3. These five statements were also used in the 2001 Survey and the 2011 QOL Survey. The composite mean score and the

Table 6.2 Statements and mean scores on Family Values

Statements on family values	Mean score (rank) 2001[1]	Mean score (rank) 2011[1]	Mean score (rank) 2016
A. Family love makes a person feel appreciated and treasured.	4.83 (1)	5.20 (4)	5.39 (4)
B. One should support one's parents in their old age.	4.76 (2)	5.28 (1)	5.40 (2)
C. Family members should stand by one another through ups and downs.	4.73 (3)	5.23 (2)	5.40 (2)
D. One should honor one's parents and grandparents.	4.70 (4)	5.23 (2)	5.43(1)
E. Family members should communicate openly and honestly with each other.	4.69 (5)	5.09 (5)	5.27 (6)
F. Family members should be prepared to make sacrifices to help each other.	4.61 (6)	5.02 (6)	5.19 (7)
G. One should strive to provide the best for one's children.	4.54 (7)	4.97 (7)	5.32 (5)
Family values (composite score)	4.69	5.15	5.34

1 Mean of 6-point sale: 1 = Strongly disagree, 6 = Strongly agree.

Table 6.3 Statements and mean scores on Eco-orientation

Statements on eco-orientation	Mean score 2001 (rank)	Mean score 2011 (rank)	Mean score 2016 (rank)
A. I would be willing to use a nonpolluting detergent even if I have my laundry less white.	4.01 (4)	4.00 (4)	4.10 (4)
B. I would be willing to bring my own bags for shopping to reduce the use of nonrecyclable bags.	3.90 (5)	4.25 (2)	4.24 (2)
C. I usually buy products that use recyclable packaging.	4.04 (3)	3.95 (5)	4.08 (5)
D. I will stop buying my favorite brand if I know the company producing it was polluting the environment.	4.12 (2)	4.34 (1)	4.43 (1)
E. I am willing to pay more for products that are friendly to the environment.	4.30 (1)	4.15 (3)	4.17 (3)
Eco-orientation (composite score)	4.03	4.03	4.20

mean scores for the individual statements for 2016 were higher than those for 2001 and 2011. However, the ranking of the mean scores in 2016 was identical to that of 2011. This result indicated that more Singaporeans continued to be appreciative of the need to protect the environment, even those who are brand conscious. It is also encouraging to note that the statement "I would be willing to bring my own bags for shopping to reduce the use of nonrecyclable bags," which was ranked last in 2001 but ranked second in 2011, continued to be ranked second in 2016. This implies that the campaign to reduce plastic waste has gained some traction.

Status Consciousness

The third factor, Status Consciousness, comprises the same five statements used in the 2001 Survey and the QOL 2011 Survey, as shown in Table 6.4. Although the mean composite score for 2016 was lower than that for 2011, we were not able to ascertain that Singaporeans are less status conscious, as the scale items were not comparable across the two surveys. Only five statements rather than seven statements were included in the factor termed Status Consciousness in 2016. However, the means of the five statements that were measured across all three years showed a decrease in 2016 compared to 2001 and 2011. Nevertheless, in 2016, Singaporeans were just as concerned about their status (ranked first in 2016) and even more focused on owning well-known brands (this value became 2nd-ranked compared to 7th and 6th in 2001 and 2011, respectively).

Volunteerism

The four statements measuring Volunteerism in the 2016 QOL Survey are shown in Table 6.5, compared to three statements in the 2001 Survey and the

Table 6.4 Statements and mean scores on Status Consciousness

Statements on status consciousness	Mean score 2001 (rank)	Mean score 2011 (rank)	Mean score 2016 (rank)
A. I like to own things that impress people.	3.94 (4)	3.33 (4)	2.88 (4)
B. I usually look out for well-known brands to reflect my status in life.	3.84 (7)	3.17 (6)	3.15 (2)
C. I admire people who own expensive homes, cars and clothes.	3.89 (5)	3.20 (5)	2.92 (3)
D. I feel good if the credit card I use gives the impression of high status with exclusives privileges.	3.85 (6)	3.03 (7)	2.57 (5)
E. My social status is an important part of my life.	4.12 (3)	3.94 (2)	3.62 (1)
F. Money can solve most people's problems	4.30 (1)	4.32 (1)	N.A.[1]
G. If I had to choose between having more money and leisure, I would choose more money.	4.24 (2)	3.94 (2)	N.A.
Status consciousness (composite score)	4.01	3.34	3.03

1 N.A.: This item was not part of the factor of Status Consciousness.

Table 6.5 Statements and means scores on Volunteerism

Statements on volunteerism	Mean score 2001 (rank)	Mean score 2011 (rank)	Mean score 2016 (rank)
A. I am willing to do volunteer work on a regular basis.	3.93 (2)	3.96 (2)	3.89 (3)
B. I often find time to be involved in community or charity work.	3.90 (3)	3.77 (3)	3.61 (4)
C. I feel I should do my part to help raise funds for charity.	4.27 (1)	4.30 (1)	4.16 (2)
D. I often donate money for charitable causes	N.A. [1]	N.A. [1]	4.17 (1)
Volunteerism (composite score)	4.03	4.01	3.96

1 N.A.: This item was not part of the factor of Volunteerism in 2001 and 2011.

2011 QOL Survey. Despite the addition of one statement, the mean composite score for Volunteerism in 2016 was lower than those in 2001 and 2011. The means and ranking of the four statements in 2016 show that Singaporeans' Volunteerism focused more on monetary contributions than on actual involvement in community work.

Traditionalism

The three statements in the 2016 Traditionalism factor that measured views about divorce, premarital sex and the importance of religion were included as part of the Conservatism factor in the 2011 QOL Survey and the 2001 Survey (see Table 6.6). Although the mean composite score for 2016 is higher than that for 2011, we cannot ascertain that Singaporeans are more traditional (or conservative) because four statements rather than three were included in the factor termed Traditionalism in 2016. However, the mean ratings and ranking for the identical three statements used for the past three years show that, in 2016, Singaporeans appeared to be more conservative than they were in 2001 and 2011. Singaporeans were traditional in terms of celebrating festivals, with a high mean score of 4.46 (out of a 6-point scale) in 2016.

Entrepreneurial Spirit

The statements measuring Entrepreneurial Spirit in the 2016 QOL Survey are shown in Table 6.7. These are similar to the ones used in the 2001 Survey and the 2011 QOL Survey. Except for "I have more self- confidence than most people," the other two indicators (mean scores for individual statements and means for composite scores) were higher in 2016 compared to 2001 and 2011, implying that Singaporeans were becoming more entrepreneurial over the years, despite losing some self-confidence.

Table 6.6 Statements and mean scores on Conservatism (2001 and 2011) and part of Traditionalism (2016)

Statements on conservatism (2001 and 2011) and traditionalism (2016)	Mean score 2001 (rank)	Mean score 2011 (rank)	Mean score 2016 (rank)
A. Divorce is unacceptable.	4.13 (2)	3.77 (3)	3.90 (4)
B. Religion is an important part of my life.	4.17 (1)	4.21 (1)	4.42 (2)
C. It is wrong to have sex before marriage	4.12 (3)	4.13 (2)	4.21 (3)
D. I celebrate festivals in the traditional way	N.A.[1]	N.A.	4.46 (1)
Conservatism/Traditionalism (composite score)	4.14	4.04	4.22

1 N.A.: This item was not part of the Conservatism factor in 2001 and 2011.

Table 6.7 Statements and mean scores on Entrepreneurial Spirit

Statements on entrepreneurial spirit	Mean score 2001 (rank)	Mean score 2011 (rank)	Mean score 2016 (rank)
A. I have more self-confidence than most people.	4.22 (1)	4.40 (1)	4.38 (3)
B. I am creative and resourceful in solving problems.	4.14 (3)	4.33 (3)	4.49 (2)
C. To me, realizing my fullest potential is more important than monetary awards.	4.22 (1)	4.37 (2)	4.68 (1)
Entrepreneurial spirit (composite score)	4.22	4.37	4.51

Table 6.8 Statements and mean scores on Materialism

Statements on materialism	Mean score 2001 (rank)	Mean score 2011 (rank)	Mean score 2016 (rank)
A. Money can solve most people's problems	4.30 (1)	4.32 (1)	4.04 (1)
B. If I had to choose between having more money and leisure, I would choose more money.	4.24 (2)	3.94 (2)	3.71 (2)
Materialism (composite score)	N.A.[1]	N.A.[1]	3.87

1 N.A.: These items were part of the factor of Status Consciousness in 2001 and 2011.

Materialism

This final and seventh factor comprises two statements relating to money that used to be part of the Status Consciousness factor in the 2001 Survey and the 2011 QOL Survey (see Table 6.8). The mean scores for the two statements on materialism have declined since 2001 and 2011, implying that Singaporeans are less pecuniary conscious over the years.

The means for the value orientations provided some insights into how the value orientations have evolved (see Tables 6.2–6.8). The means for all the value orientations have increased over the years, except for Status Consciousness and Volunteerism.

Identification of clusters

Based on the seven factors identified, a *k*-means cluster analysis was conducted to identify groups of Singaporeans based on their responses to the various statements on value orientations. These clusters should be stable and reproducible according to accepted statistical protocol. We are also interested in exploring how the 2016 clusters are different from the clusters in the 2001 and 2011 studies. Our analyses showed that a five-cluster solution provided good interpretability and also comparability with the 2011 six-cluster solution. An ANOVA shows that all F ratios that describe the differences between clusters were statistically significant, hence indicating that the seven factors contributed much to the separation of the clusters. Figure 6.1 shows the radar diagram of the five clusters

Figure 6.1 Five clusters of Singaporeans

Table 6.9 Cluster centroids

Values	Cluster 1[1]	Cluster 2	Cluster 3	Cluster 4	Cluster 5
Family values	0.42828 (2)	0.19599 (3)	–0.46330 (4)	–0.62940 (5)	0.49213 (1)
Eco-orientation	0.52288 (2)	0.31799 (3)	–0.74223 (4)	–0.78362 (5)	0.54139 (1)
Status consciousness	–0.80416 (5)	0.26569 (2)	–0.11718 (3)	–0.13653 (4)	0.87355 (1)
Traditionalism	0.36468 (3)	–0.95201 (5)	–0.73551 (4)	0.52389 (2)	0.75534 (1)
Entrepreneurial spirit	0.21960 (3)	–0.01673 (4)	–1.28224 (5)	0.39395 (2)	0.61298 (1)
Materialism	–01.08153 (5)	0.22082 (2)	0.19758 (3)	0.12402 (4)	0.69905 (1)
Volunteerism	0.48811 (2)	0.21973 (3)	–0.70841 (4)	–0.93361 (5)	0.78166 (1)
Number of cases (Total =1496 excluding 7 outliers)	336 (22.4%)	301 (20.1%)	282 (18.9%)	281 (18.8%)	296 (19.8%)

1 Numbers in brackets indicate rank according to the value of the centroids.

and the extent to which each value orientation is manifested in each of these clusters. Table 6.9 shows the cluster centroids, which, together with the demographics shown in Table 6.10, are used in describing the clusters in greater detail.

Description of clusters

Cluster 1: The Pro-Social Family-Oriented

This cluster included 22.4 percent of Singaporeans. They had the second highest score on Family Values, Eco-orientation, and Volunteerism, indicating a strong focus on family and also an outward-looking perspective in terms of caring for others and the environment. They were average on Traditionalism and Entrepreneurial Spirit (3rd-ranked on both value orientations) and the least materialistic and status conscious (lowest scores on Materialism and Status Consciousness). We have labeled this cluster The Pro-Social Family-Oriented.

Demographically, as shown in Table 6.10, this group comprised slightly more females (62 percent). Most of the members in this cluster came from an older age group of 45 to 54 years (21.1 percent). They were mostly married (70.5 percent), with more Malays than the total sample (19.9 percent versus 14 percent). A majority of them had secondary/junior college/polytechnic educations (60.7 percent) and household incomes between S$3001 and S$8000 (39.2 percent).

Cluster 2: The Status-Conscious

This cluster included 20.1 percent of Singaporeans. They had the second highest scores on Status Consciousness and Materialism, thus the naming of the cluster as The Status-Conscious. They had the lowest score on Traditonalism and the second lowest score on Entrepreneurial Spirit. They were average on Family Values, Eco-orientation and Volunteerism (3rd-ranked on all three value orientations).

Demographically, as shown in Table 6.10, this group's members were quite gender-balanced (48.2 percent male versus 51.8 percent female) and younger than the first cluster as almost a quarter each were from the 15- to 24-year, 25- to 34-year and 35- to 44-year age groups (20.6 percent, 20.3 percent and 25.6 percent, respectively). There was a higher proportion of singles (44 percent versus 33 percent for the total sample), and more Chinese (88.7 percent versus 76.3 percent for the total sample). Half of the Singaporeans in this cluster had secondary/junior college/polytechnic educations (53.2 percent), while more than a third were graduates (40.2 percent). Slightly more than a third (37.5 percent) had household incomes between S$3001 to S$8000, and more than a quarter (28.4 percent) of them had higher incomes of S$8001 to S$15,000.

Cluster 3: The Dreamers

This cluster included 18.9 percent of Singaporeans. They had the lowest score on Entrepreneurial Spirit and the second lowest scores on Family Values, Eco-orientation, Traditionalism, and Volunteerism. They were average on Status Consciousness and Materialism (3rd-ranked on these two values). As the scores were relatively low across the various value orientations with no strong distinctive characteristics, we have labeled this as The Dreamers.

Demographically, as shown in Table 6.10, this group's members were also quite gender-balanced (49.3 percent male versus 50.7 percent female). They were fairly well distributed across all age groups, from the 15- to 24-years age group to 65 years and above. Close to two-thirds were married (60.4 percent), and most were Chinese (89 percent versus 76.3 percent for the total sample). More than half of Singaporeans in this cluster had secondary/junior college/ polytechnic (52.2 percent) educations. Slightly more than a third of the Singaporeans in this cluster (37.3 percent) had household incomes of less than S$3000, and another third (33.5 percent) had household incomes between S$3001 and S$8000.

Cluster 4: The Traditional Entrepreneurs

This cluster included 18.8 percent of Singaporeans. They had the second highest scores on Traditionalism and Entrepreneurial Spirit, the second lowest scores on Materialism and Status Consciousness, and the lowest scores on Family

Table 6.10 Demographic profiles of clusters

Demographics	Cluster 1	Cluster 2	Cluster 3	Cluster 4	Cluster 5	Total
Base	336	301	282	281	296	1496[1]
Gender						
Male	128 (38%)	145 (48.2%)	139 (49.3%)	160 (57%)	154 (52%)	726
Female	208 (62%)	156 (51.8%)	143 (50.7%)	121 (43%)	142 (48%)	770
Age group						
15–24	41 (12.2%)	62 (20.6%)	44 (15.6%)	21 (7.5%)	57 (19.3%)	225
25–34	51 (15.2%)	61 (20.3%)	54 (19.1%)	40 (14.2%)	43 (14.5%)	249
35–44	61 (18.2%)	77 (25.6%)	49 (17.4%)	53 (18.9%)	53 (17.9%)	293
45–54	74 (21.1%)	50 (16.6%)	42 (15%)	48 (17.1%)	73 (24.7%)	287
55–64	65 (19.3%)	34 (11.3%)	43 (15.2%)	61 (21.7%)	37 (12.5%)	240
65 and above	44 (13.1%)	17 (5.6%)	50 (17.7%)	58 (20.6%)	33 (11.1%)	202
Marital status[2]						
Single	91 (29.5%)	120 (44%)	101 (39.6%)	57 (21.7%)	83 (31%)	452 (33%)
Married	217 (70.5%)	153 (56%)	154 (60.4%)	206 (78.3%)	189 (69%)	919 (67%)
Total	308	273	255	263	272	1371
Ethnic origin						
Chinese	232 (69.1%)	267 (88.7%)	251 (89%)	216 (76.9%)	175 (59%)	1141 (76.3%)
Malay	67 (19.9%)	15 (5%)	18 (6.4%)	35 (12.5%)	74 (25%)	209 (14%)
Indian	30 (8.9%)	14 (4.6%)	9 (3.2%)	26 (9.2%)	38 (13%)	117 (7.8%)
Others	7 (2.1%)	5 (1.7%)	4 (1.4%)	4 (1.4%)	9 (3%)	29 (1.9%)
Education						
Primary and below	35 (10.4%)	20 (6.6%)	65 (23%)	76 (27%)	23 (7.8%)	219 (14.6%)
Secondary/ Vocational/junior college/Polytechnic	204 (60.7%)	160 (53.2%)	147 (52.2%)	148 (53%)	203 (68.6%)	862 (57.6%)
University/ postgraduate	97 (28.9%)	121 (40.2%)	70 (24.8%)	57 (20%)	70 (23.6%)	415 (27.8%)

(*Continued*)

Table 6.10 (Continued)

Demographics	Cluster 1	Cluster 2	Cluster 3	Cluster 4	Cluster 5	Total
Monthly household income[3]						
Less than S$3000	78 (34.4%)	52 (25%)	69 (37.3%)	70 (57%)	81 (42%)	350 (37.4%)
S$3001–S$8000	89 (39.2%)	78 (37.5%)	62 (33.5%)	30 (24.4%)	78 (40.4%)	337 (36%)
S$8001–S$15,000	39 (17.2%)	59 (28.4%)	36 (19.5%)	18 (14.6%)	21 (10.9%)	173 (18.5%)
S$15,001 and above	21 (9.2%)	19 (9.1%)	18 (9.7%)	5 (4%)	13 (6.7%)	76 (8.1%)
Total	227	208	185	123	193	936

1 Total does not add up to 1503 due to deletion of 7 outliers.
2 Total does not add up to the respective cluster numbers as other marital statuses are noted as missing.
3 Total does not add up to the respective cluster numbers as others who did not disclose income are excluded.

Values, Eco-orientation and Volunteerism. Hence we have labeled them The Traditional Entrepreneurs.

Demographically, as shown in Table 6.10, this group's members were mostly male (57 percent) and slightly older, with close to a quarter from the 55- to 64-year age group. More than three-quarters of them were married (78.3 percent), and the distribution across the four races is close to the the total sample, with Chinese being the majority. More than half had secondary/junior college/polytechic educations (53 percent), although compared to the previous three clusters, this cluster had a higher percentage (27 percent) with primary and below educations. Household incomes for this cluster were low, with half (57 percent) having incomes of less than S$3000.

Cluster 5: The Materialistic Family-Oriented

This cluster included 19.8 percent of Singaporeans. They had the highest scores on all seven value orientations, namely Family Values, Eco-orientation, Status Consciousness, Traditionalism, Entrepreneurial Spirit, Materialism and Volunteerism. They were one of two highly family-oriented clusters and were different from the Pro-Social Family-Oriented cluster due to their materialistic leanings. Hence we have labeled them The Materialistic Family-Oriented.

Demographically, as shown in Table 6.10, this group's members were quite equally distributed across both genders (52 percent male and 48 percent female), and a quarter (27.4 percent) from the 45- to 54-year age group. More than two-thirds (69 percent) were married Singaporeans. This cluster was more ethnically diverse, with more Malays (25 percent), Indian (13 percent) and others (3 percent), and fewer Chinese (59 percent) than the total sample. Also, more than two-thirds of Singaporeans in this cluster had secondary/junior college/polytechnic educations (68.6 percent), which was the highest across the five clusters and also above that for the total sample (57.6 percent). It had more Singaporeans in the less than S$3000 household income range (42 percent) and in the S$3001 to S$8000 range, compared to the total sample (37.4 percent and 36 percent, respectively). This cluster had attained a good level of education, although the incomes were in the lower range.

Comparisons of clusters: 2001, 2011 and 2016

In the following section, comparisons are made between the eight clusters of 2001, the six clusters of 2011 and the five clusters of 2016 (Figure 6.2) to shed light on the evolving value orientations of Singaporeans. The revision in the number and composition of the clusters in 2016 could be partly attributed to the changes in the factors/value orientations used in the clustering exercise. As mentioned, out of the seven factors, only three factors (Family Values, Eco-orientation, and Entrepreneurial Spirit) retained the same items as those used in the 2011 QOL Survey.

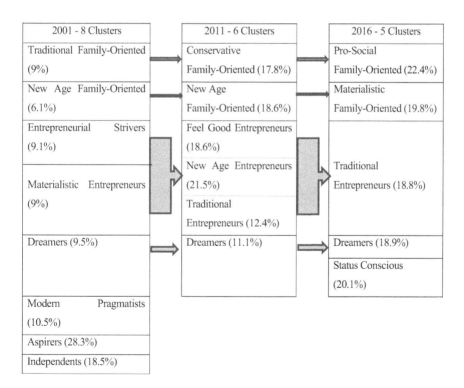

Figure 6.2 Comparisons of clusters: 2001, 2011 and 2016

In 2016, we saw some interesting developments in the five-cluster configuration. Family Values continued to feature strongly. There were two family-oriented clusters, and they were differentiated by their views on Status Consciousness and Materialism. In previous years, we also had family-oriented clusters, but they were distinguished by their views on Traditionalism/Conservatism and Eco-orientation/Volunteerism. The interesting cluster that has appeared was the Materialistic Family-Oriented cluster, which had top scores for all the value orientations. This was an "all-rounder" type of cluster that seemed to want and/or strive for everything.

Similar to 2011, the Traditional Entrepreneurs cluster remained. However, in 2016, there was only one cluster of entrepreneurs compared to the three clusters in 2011. Previously, Eco-orientation and Volunteerism were used to distinguish among the three clusters. However, in 2016, we noted that these value orientations were more diffuse across all the clusters.

The Dreamers cluster resurfaced in 2016 (18.9 percent) and was a larger cluster compared to 2001 (9.5 percent) and 2011 (11.1 percent). The 2016 and 2011 clusters were similar in terms of their lowest scores on entrepreneurial spirit.

A Status-Conscious cluster has remained through the years. The emphasis on Status Consciousness and Materialism can be seen in 2001's clusters –The Materialistic Entrepreneurs, The Dreamers and The Aspirers – and to a certain extent in 2011's cluster of The Dreamers. This emphasis appeared to be more pronounced in earlier years.

Conclusion

In this chapter, we reported the value orientations and clustering of Singaporeans in 2016 with comparisons to findings from the 2001 and 2011 surveys. Three out of the seven factors in the 2016 QOL Survey were identical to their counterparts in 2011 and were measured by the same statements on value orientations. These three factors were Family Values, Eco-orientation and Entrepreneurial Spirit. Another three factors in 2016 retained some of the statements used for their counterparts in 2011. The Status Consciousness factor now included all statements relating to status, while the two statements relating to money in the Status Consciousness factor in the 2011 QOL Survey formed the Materialism factor in 2016. The factors Volunteerism and Traditionalism, with five and four statements, respectively, have become more focused compared to the respective Volunteerism and Conservatism factors in 2011. Hence, there was some stability in the value orientations being measured as most of the items within each of the seven value orientations remained about the same over the years (2016 compared to 2011 and 2001).

Ronald Inglehart and Christian Welzel, in their analysis of the World Values Survey data, suggested that there were two major dimensions of cross-cultural variation in the world: (1) Traditional values versus Secular-rational values and (2) Survival values versus Self-expression values. Traditional values emphasize the importance of religion, parent–child ties, deference to authority and traditional family values. These societies also tend to be nationalistic. In contrast, societies embracing Secular-rational values are more open to and accepting of issues such as divorce, abortion, euthanasia and suicide. Survival values are related to economic and physical security, a relatively ethnocentric outlook and low levels of trust and tolerance. Self-expression values give high priority to environmental protection, a tolerance of marginalized groups and demands for participation in decision making in economic and political life.

Singaporeans' strong emphasis on Family Values and Traditionalism would place Singapore on the Traditional values dimension. The focus of Singaporeans on Materialism, Eco-orientation and Entrepreneurial Spirit would also fit in with the Survival values dimension. However, it remains to be seen if having a Survival values orientation implies that Singaporeans have low levels of trust; trust and social capital will be discussed in Chapter 7.

With a fairly similar set of value orientations, we started with eight clusters in 2001, and these were narrowed down to six clusters in 2011 and finally to five clusters in 2016. The revision in the number and composition of the clusters over the years could be partly attributed to the changes in the compositions of the value orientations mentioned earlier, shifts in the scores respondents gave to each value item, and changes in the demographics of the respondents.

References

Nunnally, J.C. (1978), *Psychometric theory*, Second Edition, New York, NY, USA: McGraw-Hill.

World Values Survey. www.worldvaluessurvey.org/WVSContents.jsp (accessed November 17, 2017).

7 Trust and social capital
Nurturing a conducive environment for wellbeing

Social capital has been defined as "connections among individuals – social networks and the norms of reciprocity and trustworthiness that arise from them" (Putnam 2000, p. 19). Many studies have examined the relationship between different dimensions of social capital and subjective wellbeing, with results generally pointing to a positive relationship between measures of social capital and subjective wellbeing (Portela et al. 2013). Putnam's (2000) definition of social capital implies that trust is an important element of social capital. Researchers have distinguished between two types of trust related to social capital: personalized trust that involves people personally known and generalized trust that goes beyond the boundaries of kinship and friendship and even beyond the boundaries of acquaintance (Stolle 1998). In fact, generalized trust is the most frequently used variable in studies on social capital (Ingelhart and Klingemann 2000; Uslaner 2002), and many studies have found a positive relationship between generalized trust and subjective wellbeing (e.g., Helliwell 2003, 2006; Helliwell and Putnam 2004; Sarracino 2010; Portela et al. 2013).

In this chapter, we examine one dimension of social capital in Singapore by looking at Singaporeans' level and variation of generalized trust and provide comparative analyses on whether certain demographic segments are more trusting than others. Finally, we investigate whether there is any relationship between Singaporeans' generalized trust and subjective wellbeing in terms of their happiness, health and life satisfaction. This will help us in understanding the impact of social capital on subjective wellbeing in Singapore.

Generalized trust

In most social surveys, the question "Do you think most people can be trusted or that you can't be too careful in dealing with people?" is often used as an indicator of generalized trust (Nieminen et al. 2008). The World Values Surveys of 1990 and 1995–1997 (see Inglehart 1997) used this question alone as a measure of generalized trust. Several recent studies have continued to use this single question to examine social trust or trust in others (e.g., Jen et al. 2010; Helliwell et al. 2014; Sarracino and Mikucka 2016; Soukiazis and Ramos 2016; Hamamura et al. 2017).

Since 1972, the U.S. General Social Surveys, in addition to the World Values Survey's single question to measure generalized trust, have used another question: "Do you think most people would try to take advantage of you if they got a chance, or would they try to be fair?" Subsequently, the European Social Surveys (Reeskens and Hooghe 2008) also added one more question to the scale used by the U.S. General Social Surveys to measure generalized trust: "Would you say that most of the time people try to be helpful or that they are mostly looking out for themselves?" Like the European Social Surveys in recent years, the ASEAN Barometer Survey 2009 (Tan and Tambyah 2013) also used three questions to measure generalized trust: "Generally, do you think most people can be trusted or that you can't be too careful in dealing with people?" "Do you think most people would try to take advantage of you if they got a chance, or would they try to be fair?" "Do you think that people generally try to be helpful or that they are mostly looking out for themselves?" The responses to the three questions were coded on a 2-point scale: "1 = most people can be trusted," "2 = you can't be too careful in dealing with people," "1 = most people would try to be fair," "2 = most people would try to take advantage of me," "1 = people generally try to be helpful," and "2 = people mostly look out for themselves."

Recent studies examining the impact of social capital on subjective wellbeing have used these three questions to measure generalized trust with good scale reliability (e.g., Portela et al. 2013; Tan and Tambyah 2013; Bartolini et al. 2015). In the 2016 QOL Survey, generalized trust was thus measured via the three questions mentioned earlier in order to provide a more precise and symmetrical treatment on the trust concept and to facilitate comparative analyses.

How trusting are Singaporeans?

In response to the first generalized trust question of whether people can generally be trusted, Table 7.1a shows that more than half (53.9 percent) of Singaporeans thought that one really needs to be wary of others, with only about a third (37.4 percent) expressing a willingness to trust others. Some Singaporeans (8.7 percent) did not really have an answer to the issue. Using data from the 2009 ASEAN Barometer Survey, Tan and Tambyah (2013) also found that slightly less than a third (31.4 percent) of Singaporeans agreed that others could be trusted.

More than half (54.6 percent) of Singaporeans considered that most people would try to be fair, with about a quarter (27.5 percent) thinking that others would try to take advantage of them (see Table 7.1b). It is interesting to note that a high percentage (17.8 percent) of Singaporeans did not have an opinion on this issue. In the 2009 ASEAN Barometer Survey, a higher percentage of Singaporeans (70.4 percent) agreed that most people would try to be fair (Tan and Tambyah 2013).

Table 7.1 Trust among Singaporeans

a. *Generally, do you think people can be trusted, or that you can't be too careful in dealing with people?*	Number	%
Most people can be trusted.	562	37.4
You can't be too careful in dealing with people. (It pays to be wary of people.)	810	53.9
Don't know.	131	8.7
Total	1503	100

b. *Do you think most people would try to take advantage of you if they got the chance, or would they try to be fair?*	Number	%
Most people would try to be fair.	821	54.6
Most people would try to take advantage of me.	414	27.5
Don't know.	268	17.8
Total	1503	100

c. *Do you think that people generally try to be helpful, or that they mostly look out for themselves?*	Number	%
People generally try to be helpful.	746	49.6
People mostly look out for themselves.	588	39.1
Don't know.	169	11.2
Total	1503	100

Less than half (49.6 percent) of Singaporeans thought others could be helpful, and a third (39.1 percent) thought people would mostly look out for themselves (see Table 7.1c). One in ten (11.2 percent) Singaporeans had no answer to this question. This pattern of response was also consistent with the response in the 2009 ASEAN Barometer Survey which found less than half (47.9 percent) of Singaporeans agreeing that others could be helpful (Tan and Tambyah 2013).

Overall, Singaporeans' responses to the three trust questions revealed that they were wary of others, did not really think others could be helpful but were willing to concede that most people would try to be fair. Comparing the results of the 2016 QOL Survey and those from the 2009 ASEAN Barometer Survey, Singaporeans' trust instincts did not seem to have improved over the years. This implies that there is room for improvement in the climate for generalized trust in Singapore.

In Chapter 6, it was mentioned that Singaporeans' orientation toward Materialism, Eco-orientation and Entrepreneurial Spirit would place Singapore on the Survival dimension of cross-cultural values. Researchers implied that countries having this orientation would most likely have low levels of trust. The aforementioned low level of generalized trust found among Singaporeans seemed to provide evidence for this implication.

We next consider the bivariate analyses of the three trust questions in pairs. As shown in Table 7.2a, the first two pairs of questions ("Generally, do you think people can be trusted, or that you can't be too careful in dealing with people?" and "Do you think that people generally try to be helpful, or that they mostly look out for themselves?") were found to be significantly and strongly correlated (χ^2 = 240.41, *df* = 1 *p*<.000, *phi* coefficient = 0.436). Among Singaporeans who thought that people can be trusted (43 percent), a large majority (81.6 percent) supported the idea that people generally try to be helpful, while the majority (62.1 percent) of those who thought that one cannot be too careful in dealing with people (57 percent) believed that people generally only look out for themselves. These findings almost mirrored the results in the analysis conducted by Tan and Tambyah (2011) using data on Singapore from the AsiaBarometer 2006 survey. In the 2006 survey, among Singaporeans who thought that people can be trusted (31.6 percent), only slightly more than half (63.8 percent) supported the idea that people generally try to be helpful, while a larger majority (75.3 percent) of those who thought that one cannot be too careful in dealing with people (68.4 percent) believed that people generally only look out for themselves (Tan and Tambyah 2011).

For the second pair of questions ("Generally, do you think people can be trusted, or that you can't be too careful in dealing with people?" and "Do you think that most people would try to take advantage of you if they got the chance, or would they try to be fair?"), Table 7.2b shows that these were also significantly and strongly correlated (χ^2 = 238.05, *df* = 1, *p*<.000, *phi* coefficient = 0.449). Among Singaporeans who thought that people can be trusted (44.5 percent), they showed overwhelming support (90.1 percent) for the idea that people generally try to be fair, while about half (52.5 percent) of those who thought that one cannot be too careful in dealing with people (55.5 percent) believed that people generally will try to take advantage of others.

For the third pair of questions ("Do you think that most people would try to take advantage of you if they got the chance, or would they try to be fair?" and "Do you think that people generally try to be helpful, or that they mostly look out for themselves?"), the correlations were the strongest (χ^2 = 315.39, *df* = 1 *p*<.000, *phi* coefficient = 0.519) as shown in Table 7.2c. About three-quarters (76 percent) of the Singaporeans who believed that most people would try to be fair (66.5 percent) also believed that people are generally helpful, while about three-quarters (78.3 percent) of those who believed that people generally will try to take advantage of others (33.5 percent) also believed that people tend to look out for themselves.

Hence, it seemed that there was a consistent pattern in terms of generalized trust among Singaporeans. Although they were not the majority, Singaporeans who believed that others could be trusted tended to support the idea that others could be helpful, whereas the majority who were wary of others tended to believe that people would take advantage of others. Meanwhile, the majority of Singaporeans who believed that people would try to be fair also believed others would try to be helpful, while the minority who thought others would try to take advantage of them overwhelmingly thought people only look out for themselves.

Table 7.2 Bivariate distribution of the generalized trust items

a. First pair of questions:

Generally, do you think people can be trusted, or that you can't be too careful in dealing with people?	Do you think that people generally try to be helpful, or that they mostly look out for themselves?			
	Try to Be helpful (%)	Look out for themselves (%)	Total (%)	N
Most people can be trusted.	81.6	18.4	43.0	543
Can't be too careful in dealing with people.	37.9	62.1	57.0	720
Total	56.7	43.3	100	
N	716	547		1263
Test statistics	$\chi^2 = 240.41$, $df = 1$ $p<.000$, *phi* coefficient = 0.436			

b. Second pair of questions:

Generally, do you think people can be trusted, or you can't be too careful in dealing with people?	Do you think that most people would try to take advantage of you if they got the chance, or would they try to be fair?			
	Try to be fair (%)	Try to take advantage (%)	Total (%)	N
Most people can be trusted.	90.1	9.9	44.5	526
Can't be too careful in dealing with people.	47.5	52.5	55.5	657
Total	66.4	33.6	100%	1183
N	786	397		
Test statistics	$\chi^2 = 238.05$, $df = 1$ $p<.000$, *phi* coefficient = 0.449			

c. Third pair of questions:

Do you think that most people would try to take advantage of you if they got the chance, or would they try to be fair?	Do you think that people generally try to be helpful, or that they mostly look out for themselves?			
	Try to be helpful (%)	Look out for themselves (%)	Total (%)	N
Most people would try to be fair.	76.0	24.0	66.5	779
Most people would try to take advantage of me.	21.7	78.3	33.5	392
Total	57.8	42.2	100%	1171
N	677	494		
Test statistics	$\chi^2 = 315.39$, $df = 1$ $p<.000$, *phi* coefficient = 0.519			

Who are the trusting Singaporeans?

We examined whether there were any demographic differences that could explain Singaporeans' generalized trust, defined in terms of responses to the three questions in the generalized trust scale. The selected demographic variables are age, education, gender, monthly household income and marital status.

As can be seen from Table 7.3, male Singaporeans who were higher educated were the most willing to think that people can be trusted (question 1), while

Table 7.3 Sources of individual differences for generalized trust

Demographics	1[1]	2[1]	3[1]
Age			
• 15–24	1.56	**1.38**	**1.49**
• 25–34	1.63	**1.42**	**1.54**
• 35–44	1.62	**1.35**	**1.45**
• 45–54	1.57	**1.29**	**1.42**
• 55–64	1.57	**1.29**	**1.37**
• 65 and above	1.58	**1.26**	**1.36**
• *F*-stats	0.89	**3.33**	**3.84**
• *p*<	N.S.	**.005**	**.002**
Education			
• Low	**1.61**	**1.35**	**1.39**
• Medium	**1.61**	**1.38**	**1.48**
• High	**1.54**	**1.25**	**1.38**
• *F*-stats	**2.79**	**9.23**	**6.32**
• *p*<	**.06**	**.000**	**.002**
Gender			
• Male	**1.56**	1.34	1.44
• Female	**1.62**	1.33	1.44
• *F*-stats	**4.71**	0.25	0.011
• *p*<	**.03**	N.S.	N.S.
Household income			
• Low	1.66	1.39	1.48
• Medium-low	1.66	1.37	**1.57**
• Medium-high	1.64	1.35	**1.43**
• High	1.55	1.26	**1.49**
• *F*-stats	1.31	1.55	**3.01**
• *p*<	N.S.	N.S.	**.03**
Marital status			
• Single	1.62	**1.39**	**1.52**
• Married	1.57	**1.30**	**1.40**
• *F*-stats	2.55	**10.71**	**16.27**
• *p*<	N.S.	**.001**	**.000**

1 Numbers refer to the three trust questions: 1 – "Generally, do you think most people can be trusted or that you can't be too careful in dealing with people?"; 2 – "Do you think most people would try to take advantage of you if they got a chance, or would they try to be fair?"; 3 – "Do you think that people generally try to be helpful, or that they mostly look out for themselves?"

N.S. = Not significant.

Bold figures indicate statistical significance.

Singaporeans who were married, older (65 years and above) and more educated were the most likely to think others can be fair. Finally, Singaporeans who are married, older (65 years and above), higher educated and earning medium-high incomes were most likely to think that others can be helpful. Thus it appears that age, education (and, relatedly, income) and marriage do enhance Singaporeans' sense of generalized trust. In a study based on the 2006 AsiaBarometer Survey, Tan and Tambyah (2011) also found that Singaporeans who were more educated, married and with higher incomes were also more trusting. In the study based on the 2009 ASEAN Barometer Survey, Tan and Tambyah (2013) found that, in Singapore, "the higher the level of education and income, the higher the trusting propensity." The positive association between education and generalized trust for Singaporeans was consistent with what other researchers have found (Knack and Keefer 1997; Newton and Norris 2000; Putnam 2000; Uslaner 2002; Marschall and Stolle 2004; Tokuda and Inoguchi 2010). On the other hand, others have found a negative association between income and trust (Stolle 1998; Delhey and Newton 2005), while Delhey and Newton (2002) found that education was not closely associated with social trust. Our finding on marital status was also consistent with what Nieminen et al. (2008) found in Finland that trust was greater among married people than those with other marital statuses. The nonsignificant association between age and the trust question of "Generally, do you think people can be trusted, or do you think that you can't be too careful in dealing with people?" that we found for Singaporeans was consistent with studies that adopted this single item measure of social trust (e.g., Delhey and Newton 2002). The presence of a significant gender effect on only one out of three generalized trust questions was not surprising, given that other studies have produced mixed evidence for the role of gender (e.g., Stolle 1998; Patterson 1999; Delhey and Newton 2002; Nieminen et al. 2008; Schyns and Koop 2010).

Does generalized trust contribute toward Singaporeans' subjective wellbeing?

A review of the literature on the impact of social trust on subjective wellbeing shows that happiness, self-reported health and life satisfaction were three common indicators of subjective wellbeing (e.g., Tokuda et al. 2010; Portela et al. 2013; Churchill and Mishra 2017; Hamamura et al. 2017; Jen et al. 2010; Growiec and Growiec 2014; Bartolini et al. 2015). Hence, we examined the impact of generalized trust on Singaporeans' subjective wellbeing using the wellbeing indicators as follows:

1 Happiness via the question, "All things considered, would you say that you are happy these days?" with answers ranging from "1 = very unhappy" to "5 = very happy"

2 Health via the question "How satisfied or dissatisfied are you with your health?" with answers ranging from "1 = very dissatisfied" to "6 = very satisfied"

3   Life satisfaction via an average of responses to the five-item Satisfaction with Life Scale by Diener et al. (1985)
4   Satisfaction with overall quality of life via the question "How satisfied or dissatisfied are you with your overall quality of life in general?" with answers ranging from "1 = very dissatisfied" to "6 = very satisfied"
5   Satisfaction with overall quality of life in Singapore via the question "How satisfied or dissatisfied are you with your overall quality of life in Singapore?" with answers ranging from "1 = very dissatisfied" to "6 = very satisfied"

The average responses to the three trust questions representing generalized trust were used as the dependent variable in regression analyses, with age, education, gender, household income and marital status as control variables.

Table 7.4 shows that generalized trust had a significant and positive impact on happiness, health and all three measures of life satisfaction. These results were consistent with what other researchers have found. Studies have found that social trust was positively related to happiness (e.g., Tokuda et al. 2010; Portela et al. 2013; Growiec and Growiec 2014; Bartolini et al. 2015; Hamamura et al. 2017), health (e.g., Jen et al. 2010; Hamamura et al. 2017) and life satisfaction (e.g., Portela et al. 2013; Bartolini et al. 2015; Hamamura et al. 2017; Churchill and Mishra 2017).

Hence, generalized trust did contribute to Singaporeans' subjective wellbeing in terms of their happiness, health and life satisfaction. Since generalized trust is an important component of social policies that encourage the development of social capital, trust thus plays an important role in enhancing Singaporeans' happiness, health and life satisfaction.

Table 7.4 The impact of generalized trust on happiness, health and life satisfaction

Dependent variables	Happiness	Health	Satisfaction with life	Satisfaction with overall quality of life	Satisfaction with overall quality of life in Singapore
Constant	1.348^3	3.618^3	2.736^3	3.6553	3.795^3
Age	0.020^3	-0.064^1	0.002	0.003	0.001
Gender	0.105	0.043	0.068	0.087	0.086
Education	0.042	−0.070	−0.067	−0.042	−0.075
Household income	0.081^1	$0.138**$	0.113^2	0.105^2	0.042
Marital status	−0.053	0.041	0.272^2	0.032	−0.032
Generalized trust	0.551^3	0.597^3	0.546^3	0.467^3	0.517^3
R^2	0.279	0.283	0.319	0.266	0.243
F-values ($p <$)	8.917^3	9.218^3	11.961^3	8.078^3	6.661^3

1 $p < .05$.
2 $p < .01$.
3 $p < .000$.

Conclusion

It has been established that the existence and maintenance of interpersonal trust was correlated with lower crime, better health and happiness, enhanced economic development, increased success of schools and their pupils, strengthened political participation and more effective governments (see Freitag 2006). Despite the fact that generalized trust was not high among Singaporeans, some Singaporeans who believed that others could be trusted tended to support the idea that others could be helpful, and the majority of Singaporeans who believed that people would try to be fair also believed that others would try to be helpful. We found that age, education (and, relatedly, income) and marriage enhanced Singaporeans' sense of generalized trust. Together with the finding that generalized trust played a significant and positive role in enhancing Singaporeans' subjective wellbeing, this implies that policies aimed at encouraging the development of social capital through education and programs that encourage social interactions would be helpful. In examining the pre- and postcrisis experience of 30 European countries between the years 2002 and 2010, researchers have found that communities and nations with better social capital and trust are able to respond more effectively to crisis and transitions (Helliwell et al. 2014). This further underscores the importance of building up generalized trust and social capital in Singapore, which is an open economy and a small country vulnerable to events happening in other parts of the world.

References

Asia Barometer Survey (2006), www.asiabarometer.org (accessed January 25, 2018).

Bartolini, S., Mikucka, M., and Sarracino, F. (2015), 'Money, trust and happiness in transition countries: Evidence from time series', *Social Indicators Research*, published online October 8, 2015. DOI 10.1007/s11205-015-1130-3.

Churchill, S., and Mishra, V. (2017), 'Trust, social networks and subjective wellbeing in China', *Social Indicators Research*, published online January 4, 2016. DOI 10.1007/s11205-015-1220-2.

Delhey, J., and Newton, K. (2002), 'Who trusts? The origins of social trust in seven nations', *WZB Discussion Paper*, No. FS III 02–402.

Delhey, J., and Newton, K. (2005), 'Predicting cross-national levels of social trust: Global pattern or Nordic exceptionalism?', *European Sociological Review*, 12(4), 311–327.

Diener, E., Emmons, R.A., Larsen, R.J., and Griffin, S. (1985), 'The satisfaction with life scale', *Journal of Personality Assessment*, 49, 71–75.

Freitag, M. (2006), 'Bowling the state back in: Political institutions and the creation of social capital', *European Journal of Political Research*, 45(1), 123–152.

Growiec, K., and Growiec, J. (2014), 'Trusting only whom you know, knowing only whom you trust: The joint impact of social capital and trust on happiness in CEE countries', *Journal of Happiness Studies*, 15, 1015–1040.

Hamamura, T., Li, L., and Chan, D. (2017), 'The association between generalized trust and physical and psychological health across societies', *Social Indicators Research*, published online August 8, 2016. DOI 10.1007/s11205-016-1428-9.

Helliwell, J.F. (2003), 'How's life? Combining individual and national variables to explain subjective wellbeing', *Economic Modelling*, 20(2), 331–360.

Helliwell, J.F. (2006), 'Well-being, social capital and public policy: What's new?', *The Economic Journal*, 116(510), 34–45.

Helliwell, J.F., Huang, H., and Wang, S. (2014), 'Social capital and well-being in times of Crisis', *Journal of Happiness Studies*, 15, 145–162.

Helliwell, J.F., and Putnam, R.D. (2004), 'The social context of well-being', *Philosophical Transactions: Royal Society of London Series Biological Sciences*, 359(1449), 1435–1446.

Inglehart, R. (1997), *Modernization and post-modernization: Cultural, economic, and political change in 43 societies*, Princeton, NJ, USA: Princeton University Press.

Ingelhart, R., and Klingemann, H.D. (2000), 'Genes, culture, democracy, and happiness', in *Culture and subjective well-being*, edited by E. Diener and E.M. Suh, Boston, MA, USA: MIT Press, 165–183.

Jen, M.H., Sund, E.R., Johnston, R., and Jones, K. (2010), 'Trustful societies, trustful individuals, and health: An analysis of self-rated health and social trust using the World Values Survey', *Health & Place*, 16, 1022–1029.

Knack, S., and Keefer, P. (1997), 'Does social capital have an economic payoff? A cross-country investigation', *Quarterly Journal of Economics*, 112, 1251–1288.

Marschall, M.J., and Stolle, D. (2004), 'Race and the city: Neighborhood context and the development of generalized trust', *Political Behavior*, 26(2), 125–153.

Newton, K., and Norris, P. (2000), 'Confidence in public institutions: Faith, culture or performance?', in *Disaffected democracies: What's troubling the trilateral countries?*, edited by S.J. Pharr and R.D. Putnam, Princeton, NJ, USA: Princeton University Press, 52–73.

Nieminen, T., Martelin, T., Koskinen, S., Simpura, J., Alanen, E., Harkanen, T., and Aromaa, A. (2008), 'Measurement and socio-demographic variation of social capital in a large population-based survey', *Social Indicators Research*, 85, 405–423.

Patterson, O. (1999), 'Liberty against the democratic state: On the historical and contemporary sources of American distrust', in *Democracy and trust*, edited by M. Warren, New York, NY, USA: Cambridge University Press, 151–207.

Portela, M., Neira, I., and Salinas-Jimenez, M. (2013), 'Social capital and subjective wellbeing in Europe: A new approach on social capital', *Social Indicators Research*, 114, 493–511.

Putnam, R. (2000), *Bowling alone: Collapse and revival of American community*, New York, NY, USA: Simon & Schuster.

Reeskens, T. and Hooghe, M. (2008), 'Cross-cultural measurement of generalized trust: Evidence from the European Social Survey (2002 and 2004)', *Social Indicators Research*, 85, 515–532.

Sarracino, F. (2010), 'Social capital and subjective wellbeing trends: Comparing 11 Western European countries', *The Journal of Socio-Economics*, 39, 482–517.

Sarracino, F., and Mikucka, M. (2016), 'Social capital in Europe from 1990 to 2012: Trends and convergence', *Social Indicators Research*, published online February 10, 2016. DOI 10.1007/s11205-016-1255-z.

Schyns, P., and Koop, C. (2010), 'Political distrust and social capital in Europe and the USA', *Social Indicators Research*, 96(1), 145–167.

Soukiazis, E., and Ramos, S. (2016), 'The structure of subjective well-being and its determinants: A micro-data study for Portugal', *Social Indicators Research*, 126, 1575–1399.

Stolle, D. (1998), 'Bowling together, bowling alone: The development of generalized trust in voluntary associations', *Political Psychology*, 19(3), 497–526.

Tan, S.J., and Tambyah, S.K. (2011), 'Generalized trust and trust in institutions in Confucian Asia', *Social Indicators Research*, 103(2), 357–377.

Tan, S.J., and Tambyah, S.K. (2013), 'Trusting propensity and trust in institutions: A comparative study of 5 ASEAN nations', in *Psychology of trust: New research*, edited by D. Gefen, New York, NY, USA: Nova Science, 281–304.

Tokuda, Y., Fuji, S., and Inoguchi, T. (2010), 'Individual and country-level effects of social trust on happiness: The Asia Barometer survey', *Journal of Applied Social Psychology*, 40(10), 2574–2593.

Uslaner, E.M. (2002), *The moral foundations of trust*, Cambridge, UK: Cambridge University Press.

8 Rights, politics and the role of the government

In the previous chapters of this book, we have explored the cognitive and affective aspects of the subjective wellbeing of Singaporeans (Chapters 2 and 3), the relationship between income and happiness in the Singaporean context (Chapter 4) and how values influence the subjective wellbeing of Singaporeans (Chapters 5 and 6). These chapters provide a multifaceted perspective of how individual-level characteristics (e.g., values) and demographics (e.g., income) are associated with subjective wellbeing. In this chapter, we will explore the association between individual-level perceptions of issues of a more macro and societal nature (e.g., democratic rights, views about politics and how the government is doing) and subjective wellbeing.

Research has suggested that citizens in democratic societies have a better sense of subjective wellbeing because democracy helps to create the conditions that contribute to subjective wellbeing, especially the opportunities for political participation. Verba and Nie (1972) defined political participation as "the means by which the interests, desires and demands of the ordinary citizens are communicated[,] . . . all those activities by private citizens that are more or less directly aimed at influencing the selection of governmental personnel and/or decisions they make" (p. 2). Political participation has been assessed in terms of the inclination or the propensity to engage in certain behaviors and/or the actual behaviors themselves. These behaviors include voting; participation in government-organized public hearings or citizens' meetings; participation in an action group; participation in a protest action, march or demonstration; working for a political campaign; contributing to a political candidate; attending a meeting or rally for a political candidate; and/or contacting an elected official within the past year. Studies have shown that there were beneficial outcomes of political participation in terms of increased trust, favorable subscription to democratic values and more participation in collective action (Putnam 2000). Teorell (2006) also suggested that political participation was a form of self-development, personal growth and fulfillment for individuals.

Despite the benefits of political participation, the evidence of its impact on wellbeing has been inconclusive (Pacheco and Lange 2010; Pirralha 2017; Weitz-Shapiro and Winters 2011). Weitz-Shapiro and Winters (2011) showed that the actual act of voting had no relationship with life satisfaction. Although

Pirralha (2017) also found no direct effect of political participation on wellbeing, he suggested that political efficacy could be a potential intervening variable between political participation and wellbeing. Specifically, he demonstrated that external political efficacy and internal political efficacy both played a role at different points in time. First, the perception of the openness of the political system (i.e., external political efficacy) had an impact on individual life satisfaction. Then, believing in one's capabilities to participate (i.e., internal political efficacy) continued to play a role in influencing individual life satisfaction. Internal political efficacy also had a larger significant effect on political participation.

Some studies have shown that the reverse relationship may hold true, for example, that happy citizens were more likely to vote and engage in other forms of political participation, which in turn perpetuates the democratic system (Barnes et al. 1979; Oishi et al. 2007; Flavin and Keane 2012). Again, the evidence has been somewhat mixed. Pirralha (2017) found no significant effect of wellbeing on political participation. Other studies have shown that satisfied citizens were less inclined to participate in protests and strikes to achieve certain policy outcomes (Barnes et al. 1979; Bahry and Silver 1990) as they were in a state of "contented idleness" (Veenhoven 1988). In contrast, Flavin and Keane (2012) showed that citizens who were satisfied were more active in turning out to vote and participate in the political process, but this participation was in activities of a nonconflictual nature (i.e., conventional political participation such as voting or giving money to political causes). Hence the link between life satisfaction and political participation may depend on the type of political activity. Similar to Pirralha (2017), Flavin and Keane (2012) suggested that the effect of life satisfaction on political participation was mediated through political efficacy (both internal and external).

As mentioned in Chapter 1, Singapore is usually classified as economically free but not politically free. If the democracy–happiness equation is valid, we might expect Singaporeans to be less happy and satisfied. However, we have shown that Singaporeans continued to be generally happy and satisfied with life, though less so with living in Singapore. They also appeared to be politically apathetic and did not seem to mind the lack of political freedom. As observed in Tambyah et al. (2010), compared to other East Asian countries like Hong Kong, Japan, South Korea, Taiwan and Singapore had one of the lowest rates of political participation. Soon (2015), noted the low levels of offline political participation during both periods of nonelection time and election time in Singapore. Less than a quarter of voters (23.5 percent) said they attended one or more political rallies during the 2015 General Election. Levels of online political participation leading up to Polling Day for the 2015 General Election were not very high either, with voters indicating that they followed a political discussion thread, a sociopolitical blogger/YouTuber or shared information and commentary "once a week or less."

Research studies on Singaporeans' views about democratic rights and politics are not common in Singapore. We have tried to address this by providing data and insights from the 2006 AsiaBarometer Survey (as reported in Tambyah et al. 2010), the 2011 QOL Survey (as reported in Tambyah and Tan 2013) and the 2016 QOL Survey (as reported in this book). Political participation was measured in the 2006 AsiaBarometer Survey but not in the 2011 QOL Survey and the 2016 QOL Survey. Instead, we use the measures related to satisfaction with democratic rights and views about politics in our analysis and discussion. We also compare some of our 2016 QOL Survey findings with surveys conducted by the Institute of Policy Studies (IPS). The first is the 2010 IPS Survey on Political Traits and Media Use (hereinafter referred to as the 2010 IPS Survey), carried out from August to October 2010 to determine the political traits of citizens and their use of and attitudes toward different forms of media. This was a national telephone survey with a representative sample of 1090 Singaporeans aged 21 years and above. The second is the 2015 IPS Survey on Internet and Media Use during GE2015 (Soon 2015). This study was based on a nationwide online survey of 2000 voters. It examined the use of mainstream and social media for the election, trust in the different types of media, political traits of voters, what they did online and offline, and their voting behavior. The third is the IPS Post-Election Survey 2015 (Koh 2015), which was done after the September 11, 2015 General Election in Singapore to examine the attitudes of voters and the factors that shaped their decisions. It had 2015 respondents who were randomly selected from a register of all land phone lines in the country. The fourth is the Perceptions of Governance Survey (Tan 2015) with a sample of 3000 voters. Respondents were asked for their views about government performance, policy issues that mattered to them, their satisfaction with life and the electoral system. General findings on these surveys were retrieved from the IPS website.

Why is the role of the government important in studies on quality of life and wellbeing? Researchers and policy makers have suggested that governments have a moral obligation to their citizens in terms of ensuring their happiness and wellbeing. For instance, Bok (2010) advocated educational reforms, measures to remove the anxiety of having no health insurance and stronger efforts to relieve the lasting distress of mental illness and unemployment as these were sources of prolonged unhappiness. As mentioned in Chapter 1, Bhutan has made Gross National Happiness an integral part of its agenda for the country. Other governments have also strived to ensure the happiness of their citizens in the implementation of policies affecting education, healthcare, housing, immigration, national security and workers' rights. In their study of happiness policy in Dutch society, Boelhouwer and van Campen (2013) found that the Dutch government was indeed a "happiness machine" that facilitated policies and programs focused on mental health and resilience for its citizens. They also suggested that governments should act as "misfortune mitigators" in societies where the average happiness levels were high and where only a few segments of citizens were unhappy and required more assistance from the government.

In the following sections, we discuss how satisfied Singaporeans are with their democratic rights, how they view various aspects of politics and the areas they would like the government to allocate more resources to. We also examine the sources of individual differences for these perceptions and the effects of these perceptions on the subjective wellbeing of Singaporeans (i.e., the overall quality of life in Singapore).

Satisfaction with democratic rights

Democratic rights include the right to vote, to participate in any kind of organization, to gather and demonstrate, to be informed about the work and functions of government, to freedom of speech and to criticize the government. Respondents were asked about their satisfaction with these rights on a scale from 1 for "very dissatisfied" to 4 for "very satisfied." Higher means indicate higher levels of satisfaction. Respondents for the 2016 QOL Survey were most satisfied with the right to vote (mean of 3.31) and most dissatisfied with the right to criticize the government (mean of 2.62). As shown in Table 8.1, all the 2016 means were higher than those for 2006 (except for freedom of speech) but lower than those for 2011. This indicates a decline in the levels of satisfaction with democratic rights over the last five years.

When we looked more closely at the means across demographic groups (see Tables 8.2 and 8.3), there were some significant differences for age. The youngest

Table 8.1 Satisfaction with democratic rights

Statement	Very dissatisfied	Somewhat dissatisfied	Somewhat satisfied	Very satisfied	Mean 2016 (rank)	Mean 2011 (rank)	Mean 2006 (rank)
	1	2	3	4			
	%	%	%	%			
The right to vote	0.9	3.1	60.1	35.9	3.31 (1)	3.57 (1)	2.99 (1)
The right to participate in any kind of organization	0.9	8.0	69.9	21.3	3.12 (2)	3.27 (2)	2.84 (2)
The right to gather and demonstrate	7.2	20.8	61.6	10.4	2.75 (4)	2.96 (4)	2.60 (4)
The right to be informed about the work and functions of government	2.5	13.8	69.2	14.5	2.96 (3)	3.12 (3)	2.45 (6)
Freedom of speech	7.0	22.4	60.7	9.9	2.74 (5)	2.88 (5)	2.79 (3)
The right to criticize the government	10.0	25.5	57.6	7.0	2.62 (6)	2.68 (6)	2.51 (5)

Table 8.2 Sources of individual differences for satisfaction with democratic rights

Demographics	The right to vote	The right to participate in any kind of organization	The right to gather and demonstrate
Age			
• 15–24	**3.20**	3.10	2.80
• 25–34	3.22	3.07	2.67
• 35–44	3.30	3.11	2.79
• 45–54	3.36	3.16	**2.83**
• 55–64	**3.40**	3.13	**2.65**
• 65 and above	3.38	3.12	2.73
• F-stats	**5.009**	0.800	**2.493**
• $p<$	**.000**	.550	**.029**
Education			
• Low	**3.43**	3.15	2.84
• Medium	**3.27**	3.09	2.72
• High	3.33	3.14	2.76
• F-Stats	**7.281**	1.846	2.257
• $p<$	**.001**	.158	.105
Gender			
• Male	3.31	3.11	2.72
• Female	3.31	3.12	2.78
• F-stats	0.107	0.181	2.527
• $p<$	.744	.670	.112
Household income[1]			
• Low	3.25	3.07	2.69
• Medium-low	3.34	3.13	2.72
• Medium-high	3.34	3.08	2.61
• High	3.39	3.13	2.73
• F-stats	2.253	0.823	0.943
• $p<$	.081	.481	.419
Marital status			
• Single	**3.24**	3.10	2.74
• Married	**3.34**	3.13	2.75
• F-stats	**8.286**	1.126	0.062
• $p<$	**.004**	.289	.804

1 Only for those 941 respondents who disclosed household income.

Bold figures indicate significance.

Table 8.3 Sources of individual differences for satisfaction with democratic rights

Demographics	The right to be informed about the work and functions of government	Freedom of speech	The right to criticize the government
Age			
• 15–24	3.01	2.63	2.52
• 25–34	**2.83**	2.57	**2.48**
• 35–44	2.95	2.73	2.62
• 45–54	**3.02**	2.83	2.68
• 55–64	2.93	2.78	2.63
• 65 and above	2.99	**2.89**	**2.77**
• *F*-stats	**3.260**	**6.580**	**4.358**
• *p*<	**.006**	**.000**	**.001**
Education			
• Low	3.04	**2.92**	**2.74**
• Medium	2.95	**2.70**	**2.57**
• High	2.92	2.71	2.64
• *F*-stats	2.469	**8.584**	**4.312**
• *p*<	.085	**.000**	**.014**
Gender			
• Male	**2.92**	2.68	2.60
• Female	**2.99**	2.79	2.63
• *F*-Stats	**4.152**	**8.002**	0.652
• *p*<	**.042**	**.005**	.419
Household income[1]			
• Low	2.94	2.72	2.58
• Medium-low	3.00	**2.78**	2.62
• Medium-high	2.88	**2.58**	2.48
• High	2.90	2.68	2.55
• *F*-Stats	1.721	**2.992**	1.250
• *p*<	.161	**.030**	.290
Marital status			
• Single	2.93	**2.67**	**2.55**
• Married	2.96	**2.76**	**2.65**
• *F*-stats	0.598	**4.561**	**5.033**
• *p*<	.439	**.033**	**.025**

1 Only for those 941 respondents who disclosed household income.

Bold figures indicate significance.

Table 8.4 Impact of satisfaction with democratic rights on satisfaction with overall quality of life in Singapore

Dependent variable: satisfaction with overall quality of life in Singapore	Unstandardized coefficients	Significance
(Constant)	2.571	0.000
The right to vote	**0.207**	**0.000**
The right to participate in any kind of organization	**0.086**	**0.045**
The right to gather and demonstrate	0.019	0.554
The right to be informed about the work and functions of government	**0.119**	**0.003**
Freedom of speech	**0.146**	**0.000**
The right to criticize the government	**0.126**	**0.000**

$R^2 = 0.194$; F value $= 59.864$; $p<.000$.

Bold figures indicate significance.

age group was the least satisfied with the right to vote, but this statistic may not be valid as only those who are 21 years of age are entitled to vote in Singapore. The 55- to 64-year age group was most satisfied with the right to vote but the least satisfied with the right to gather and demonstrate. The 25- to 34-year age group was the most disgruntled in the most categories with the lowest satisfaction means for three rights (to be informed about the work and functions of government, to have freedom of speech and to criticize the government).

In contrast, the low-education group were the most satisfied with three out of four rights, with the means for four rights being statistically higher than other groups (to vote, freedom of speech and to criticize the government). The medium-education group was most dissatisfied with three rights (to vote, freedom of speech and to criticize the government). Females were generally more satisfied with their rights than males, although the significant differences were for the right to be informed about the work and functions of government and freedom of speech.

Those with medium-high household incomes were the least satisfied with freedom of speech, while those with medium-low incomes were most satisfied with freedom of speech. Married respondents were more satisfied than single respondents. The statistically significant differences were for the right to vote, freedom of speech and to criticize the government.

In terms of the impact of satisfaction with democratic rights on satisfaction with the overall quality of life in Singapore, all the rights have a statistically significant and positive impact except for the right to gather and demonstrate. Looking again at Table 8.2, for the right to gather and demonstrate, there were no statistically significant differences among the demographic groups except for the age groups. The 45- to 54-year age group was the most dissatisfied about this right. However, it may not have an impact on their satisfaction with the overall quality of life in Singapore.

Views about politics

In the 2016 QOL Survey, we asked Singaporeans for their views about politics on a scale of "1 = strongly disagree" to "5 = strongly agree." These views about politics were described in seven statements that covered various aspects of politics such as the efficacy of voting, the empowerment of voters, and the empathy and integrity of elected officials. Higher means indicate more agreement with the statement. Care should be taken in the interpretation of the means, taking into account the opinions expressed in the statement about a particular aspect of politics. The percentages of agreement or disagreement also provided additional insights. These statistics will be described and discussed in more detail in the following sections, with comparisons to data from the 2006 AsiaBarometer Survey (Tambyah et al. 2010) and the 2011 QOL Survey (Tambyah and Tan 2013).

The efficacy of voting

As shown in Table 8.5, Singaporeans generally take their voting duties seriously as voting is compulsory in Singapore, and there are penalties for failing to turn up to vote. However, a lower percentage "strongly agreed" with the statement that "citizens have a duty to vote in elections" in 2016 (27.9 percent compared to 38.9 percent in 2011 and 51.9 percent in 2006). The mean response (4.22) was also the lowest in ten years. Those with high levels of education (mean of 4.26) and medium-high incomes (mean of 4.35) and who were 35 to 44 years of age (mean of 4.28) tended to agree more about their duty as citizens to vote, and these differences were statistically significant (see Table 8.6). Those with low levels of education (mean of 4.10) and low incomes (mean of 4.18) and who were in the 25- to 34-year age group (mean of 4.14) were more apathetic.

More Singaporeans in 2016 "agreed" (25.2 percent) with the statement that "since so many people vote in elections, it really doesn't matter whether I vote or not" compared to 2011 (19.2 percent) and 2006 (13.9 percent).

Table 8.5 The efficacy of voting

Statement	Strongly disagree 1	Disagree 2	Neither agree nor disagree 3	Agree 4	Strongly agree 5	Mean
	%	%	%	%	%	
Citizens have a duty to vote in elections.	0.1 (0.7) [0.0]	0.2 (0.6) [0.7]	5.7 (4.2) [1.5]	66.1 (55.7) [45.9]	27.9 (38.9) [51.9]	4.22 (4.31) [4.26]
Since so many people vote in elections, it really doesn't matter whether I vote or not.	12.9 (11.4) [15.7]	39.1 (47.3) [50.4]	19.5 (15.5) [18.1]	25.2 (19.2) [13.9]	3.3 (6.5) [1.9]	2.67 (2.62) [2.56]

Note: The first set of numbers in (parentheses) are from the 2011 QOL Survey as reported in Tambyah and Tan (2013). The second set of numbers in [parentheses] are from the 2006 AsiaBarometer Survey as reported in Tambyah et al. (2010).

Table 8.6 Sources of individual differences for the efficacy of voting

Demographics	Citizens have a duty to vote in elections.	Since so many people vote in elections, it really doesn't matter whether I vote or not.
Age		
• 15–24	4.24	2.67
• 25–34	**4.14**	2.78
• 35–44	**4.28**	2.57
• 45–54	4.21	2.70
• 55–64	4.24	2.63
• 65 and above	4.18	2.68
• F-stats	**2.094**	1.197
• p<	**.064**	.308
Education		
• Low	**4.10**	**2.94**
• Medium	4.23	2.73
• High	**4.26**	**2.40**
• F-stats	**5.727**	**21.218**
• p<	**.003**	**.000**
Gender		
• Male	4.23	2.66
• Female	4.20	2.67
• F-stats	0.699	0.042
• p<	.403	.838
Household income*		
• Low	**4.18**	**2.82**
• Medium-low	4.30	2.41
• Medium-high	**4.35**	2.24
• High	4.22	**2.14**
• F-stats	**4.674**	**18.170**
• p<	**.003**	**.000**
Marital status		
• Single	4.20	2.61
• Married	4.22	2.70
• F-stats	0.171	1.718
• p<	.679	.190

* Only for those 941 respondents who disclosed household income.

Bold figures indicate significance.

The mean of 2.67 was also higher than 2011 and 2006, which suggested more skepticism (see Table 8.5). Significant differences were noted for age, education and household income (see Table 8.6). Those who had low levels of education (mean of 2.94) and low incomes (mean of 2.82) were more doubtful about the efficacy of voting. Respondents who were 35 to 44 years of age (mean of 2.57) were more likely to feel that their votes counted compared to other age groups, while those who were 25 to 34 years of age (mean of 2.78) were more skeptical. However, the differences due to age were not statistically significant.

The empowerment of the voters

While Singaporeans took the duty of voting seriously, they were more ambivalent about the instrumentality of their votes. Their sense of agency was captured in the statements about whether they believed that they had the power to influence policy or actions and whether they felt they understood what was going on in the political realm (see Table 8.7). In 2016, about 58 percent of Singaporeans (11.2 percent "strongly agree" and 46.7 percent "agree") felt less politically empowered. This was similar to 2011 except for a slight shift of percentages in the two response categories (16.6 percent "strongly agree" and 41.4 "agree"). In terms of political awareness in 2016, about 54 percent of Singaporeans agreed (46.4 percent) and strongly agreed (7.7 percent) that politics was too complicated for them. This was an increase of four percentage points from 2011, suggesting more apathy. About three in ten Singaporeans (29.1 percent) also took the middle ground approach, an increase of about seven percentage points compared to 2011.

The 2010 IPS Survey assessed political efficacy among Singaporeans in terms of the extent to which people thought that they were qualified to participate in politics. Most of the respondents in the 2010 IPS Survey were in the "neither inefficacious nor efficacious" bracket (mean of 2.93, on a scale of 1 to 5). Six years on, it appears that many Singaporeans still do not feel confident about their capacity to participate in the political arena, although the two studies are not directly comparable.

Significant differences were noted for age, education, gender and household income (see Table 8.8). The 25- to 34-year age group (mean of 3.70) was most disenfranchised about their power to influence the government, while those who were 45 to 54 years old felt more empowered (mean of 3.46). Females (mean of 3.52) and those aged 65 years and above (mean of 3.57) were more likely to feel that they could not comprehend politics. Males (mean of 3.34) and respondents in the age group of 35 to 44 years (mean of 3.32) felt more confident about understanding politics. Those with medium levels of education (mean of 3.64) and low incomes (mean of 3.66) felt less empowered to influence the government. Those with low levels of education (mean of 3.66) and low incomes (mean of 3.61) felt they could not understand politics.

Table 8.7 The empowerment of voters

Statement	Strongly disagree 1	Disagree 2	Neither agree nor disagree 3	Agree 4	Strongly agree 5	Mean
	%	%	%	%	%	
Generally speaking, people like me don't have the power to influence government policy or actions.	1.0 (1.9) [1.4]	11.6 (18.2) [18.9]	29.5 (21.9) [23.4]	46.7 (41.4) [43.5]	11.2 (16.6) [12.8]	3.55 (3.53) [3.51]
Politics and government are so complicated that sometimes I don't understand what's happening.	1.3 (2.1) [1.6]	15.4 (25.9) [22.9]	29.1 (21.6) [26.9]	46.4 (37.3) [40.2]	7.7 (13.1) [8.4]	3.44 (3.33) [3.51]

Note: The first set of numbers in (parentheses) are from the 2011 QOL Survey as reported in Tambyah and Tan (2013). The second set of numbers in [parentheses] are from the 2006 AsiaBarometer Survey as reported in Tambyah et al. (2010).

The empathy and integrity of government officials

Table 8.9 shows the agreement with statements that reflect the respondents' opinions about government officials. On the whole, the means for 2016 were lower, indicating less skepticism. However, the percentages for "neither agree nor disagree" for 2016 were higher, and there were more respondents who did not have a strong opinion on these issues. The statement "There is widespread corruption among those who govern the country" measures the people's perception of the integrity of the government. Many Singaporeans continued to believe in the honesty of their government. There was a dip of about four percentage points in those disagreeing (27.9 percent in 2016 compared to 31.9 percent in 2011) about the pervasiveness of corruption as a social-political problem.

Perceptions about the engagement of the government with the people were not so favorable in 2011. The 2010 IPS Survey found that close to a third (30.2 percent) of the young adults polled believed that politicians were more concerned with having power than serving the public. However, there seemed to be a slight improvement in 2016. Close to 33 percent of Singaporeans (4.0 percent "strongly agree" and 28.8 percent "agree") felt that the government had become indifferent to their concerns after being elected; this was a drop of at least eight percentage points from 2011. Another 39 percent felt that the government officials were not sympathetic to their views (5.7 percent "strongly agree" and 33.3 percent "agree"). This was a decrease of 12 percentage points from 2011.

Significant differences were found for age, education, gender, household income and marital status (see Table 8.10). Those who were the most skeptical about the prevalence of corruption were the 25- to 34-year age group (mean of 3.02), those with medium levels of education (mean of 2.89) and low incomes

Table 8.8 Sources of individual differences for the empowerment of voters

Demographics	Generally speaking, people like me don't have the power to influence government policy or actions.	Politics and government are so complicated that sometimes I don't understand what's happening.
Age		
• 15–24	3.53	3.52
• 25–34	**3.70**	3.49
• 35–44	3.52	**3.32**
• 45–54	**3.46**	3.36
• 55–64	3.58	3.43
• 65 and above	3.56	3.57
• *F*-stats	**2.247**	**3.000**
• *p*<	.047	.011
Education		
• Low	3.56	**3.66**
• Medium	**3.64**	3.50
• High	3.37	3.17
• *F*-stats	**13.572**	**29.012**
• *p*<	**.000**	**.000**
Gender		
• Male	3.57	**3.34**
• Female	3.54	**3.52**
• *F*-stats	0.490	**15.340**
• *p*<	.484	**.000**
Household income[1]		
• Low	**3.66**	**3.61**
• Medium-low	3.55	3.32
• Medium-high	3.52	3.29
• High	**3.21**	2.96
• *F*-stats	**5.659**	**13.942**
• *p*<	**.001**	**.000**
Marital status		
• Single	3.58	3.47
• Married	3.55	3.41
• *F*-stats	0.341	1.368
• *p*<	.559	.242

1 Only for those 941 respondents who disclosed household income.

Bold figures indicate significance.

Table 8.9 Perceived empathy and integrity of government officials

Statement	Strongly disagree 1	Disagree 2	Neither agree nor disagree 3	Agree 4	Strongly agree 5	Mean
	%	%	%	%	%	
There is widespread corruption among those who govern the country.	7.7 (6.3) [9.8]	27.9 (31.9) [44.5]	46.0 (27.3) [30.0]	15.7 (27.2) [13.3]	2.7 (7.3) [2.4]	2.78 (2.97) [3.57]
Generally speaking, the people who are elected to the Singapore Parliament stop thinking about the public once they're elected.	3.4 (3.6) [2.5]	26.1 (24.7) [32.1]	37.7 (30.3) [35.8]	28.8 (30.8) [23.0]	4.0 (10.5) [6.5]	3.04 (3.20) [3.40]
Government officials pay little attention to what citizens like me think.	1.9 (2.7) [1.5]	24.6 (20.4) [25.4]	34.6 (25.8) [32.7]	33.3 (37.8) [32.9]	5.7 (13.2) [7.4]	3.16 (3.39) [3.48]

Note: The first set of numbers in (parentheses) are from the 2011 QOL Survey as reported in Tambyah and Tan (2013). The second set of numbers in [parentheses] are from the 2006 AsiaBarometer Survey as reported in Tambyah et al. (2010).

(mean of 2.88) and the singles (mean of 2.82). Those who were the least skeptical were the older respondents aged 55 to 64 years (mean of 2.58), those with high levels of education (mean of 2.60) and high incomes (mean of 2.39) and the marrieds (mean of 2.72).

Generally, those who were more educated and earning more were more confident about the government's integrity and concern for its citizens. In contrast, those who had medium levels of education and earning low or medium-low incomes were less confident about the government. The age effect was more varied. Respondents in the age group of 25 to 34 years (mean of 3.30) felt more strongly that the elected officials had stopped thinking about and neglected the electorate. Males (mean of 3.10) and low-income earners (mean of 3.0) also shared this sentiment. In contrast, respondents who were 65 years old and above (mean of 2.87), females (mean of 2.98) and high-income earners (mean of 2.75) felt that the government officials were still empathetic.

In terms of the government paying attention to its citizens, those aged 25 to 34 years (mean of 3.41), those with medium levels of education (mean of 3.23), males (mean of 3.21) and low-income earners (mean of 3.20) were more skeptical of this aspect of politics. Those aged 55 to 64 years (mean of 3.08), those with high levels of education (mean of 3.04), females (mean of 3.12) and high-income earners (mean of 2.82) were less skeptical.

The 2010 IPS Survey found that one out of every three Singaporeans distrusted politicians, with males being more politically cynical than females. We also noted the gender difference in the 2016 QOL Survey. Although the 2010 IPS Survey did not find significant differences in terms of age, income or education, the data from the 2016 QOL Survey suggested some variations for these demographics as noted in our preceding discussion.

Table 8.10 Sources of individual differences for perceived empathy and integrity of government officials

Demographics	There is widespread corruption among those who govern the country.	Generally speaking, the people who are elected to the Singapore Parliament stop thinking about the public once they're elected.	Government officials pay little attention to what citizens like me think.
Age			
• 15–24	2.93	3.01	3.16
• 25–34	**3.02**	**3.30**	**3.41**
• 35–44	2.76	3.05	3.10
• 45–54	2.75	3.00	3.11
• 55–64	**2.58**	2.96	**3.08**
• 65 and above	2.61	**2.87**	3.12
• *F*-stats	**9.221**	5.772	4.400
• *p*<	**.000**	**.000**	**.001**
Education			
• Low	2.67	2.97	3.14
• Medium	**2.89**	3.08	**3.23**
• High	**2.60**	2.99	**3.04**
• *F*-stats	**16.115**	2.242	6.182
• *p*<	**.000**	.107	**.002**
Gender			
• Male	2.74	**3.10**	**3.21**
• Female	2.81	**2.98**	**3.12**
• *F*-stats	2.716	5.670	3.778
• *p*<	.100	**.017**	**.052**
Household income[1]			
• Low	**2.88**	**3.00**	**3.20**
• Medium-low	2.73	2.93	3.04
• Medium-high	2.60	2.86	3.06
• High	**2.39**	**2.75**	**2.82**
• *F*-stats	**7.781**	2.021	4.164
• *p*<	**.000**	.109	**.006**
Marital status			
• Single	2.82	3.06	3.15
• Married	2.72	3.05	3.18
• *F*-stats	**9.156**	0.010	0.220
• *p*<	**.003**	.920	.639

1 Only for those 941 respondents who disclosed household income.

Bold figures indicate significance.

Table 8.11 Impact of views about politics on satisfaction with overall quality of life in Singapore

Dependent variable: satisfaction with overall quality of life in Singapore	Unstandardized coefficients	Significance
(Constant)	4.111	0.000
Citizens have a duty to vote in elections.	**0.257**	**0.000**
There is widespread corruption among those who govern the country. (R)	−0.30	0.207
Generally speaking, people like me don't have the power to influence government policy or actions. (R)	−0.073	**0.004**
Politics and government are so complicated that sometimes I don't understand what's happening. (R)	**0.082**	**0.001**
Since so many people vote in elections, it really doesn't matter whether I vote or not. (R)	**0.131**	**0.001**
Generally speaking, the people who are elected to the Singapore Parliament stop thinking about the public once they're elected. (R)	−0.104	**0.000**
Government officials pay little attention to what citizens like me think. (R)	−0.161	**0.000**

R = Reverse-coded statement.

Bold figures indicate significance.

To examine how Singaporeans' views about politics are correlated with Singaporeans' satisfaction with the overall quality of life in Singapore, we conducted a regression analysis, using responses to the seven statements on Views about Politics as independent variables and the Satisfaction with Overall Quality of Life in Singapore as the dependent variable. To reduce response bias, statements 2 to 7 in the statements of Views about Politics were reverse-coded for this analysis. Table 8.11 shows the results of the regression analysis ($R^2 = 0.121$; F value = 29.461; $p<.000$).

As shown in Table 8.11, having a duty to vote, a good understanding of politics and the efficacy of their votes had a positive impact on Singaporeans' satisfaction with the overall quality of life in Singapore. On the other hand, there was a negative impact on Singaporeans' satisfaction with the overall quality of life in Singapore when voters felt that they could not influence government policy or actions and when government officials do not care about or pay attention to the citizens.

Role of the government

Eleven statements on the role of the government were included in the 2011 QOL Survey. These statements covered a wide range of areas in which the government could be expected to play an active role in terms of providing funding, leadership and other means of support. For the 2016 QOL Survey, we expanded the list to 20 statements. We wanted to cover more areas that the government could participate in based on a review of current societal concerns in Singapore. We also wanted to ensure a closer match between the role of the government and other questions in the 2016 QOL Survey that asked about satisfaction with living in Singapore. This is to enable more nuanced analyses and interpretations.

In the 2016 QOL Survey, we asked Singaporeans to rate on a scale of "1 = strongly agree" to "5 = strongly disagree" on 20 statements about the role of the government. Table 8.12 shows the results and the rankings based on mean responses. Statements 1 to 8 and 10 are the same as those asked in the 2011 QOL Survey, while statements 9 and 11 to 20 are new. As indicated by the figures in bold for Table 8.12, Singaporeans placed a high priority on the government's role in the top five areas of (1) addressing the needs of the ageing population, (2) moderating rising prices, (3) helping the marginalized in society, (4) improving the public transport system and (5) providing more resources for the healthcare needs of the population. Except for the new statements relating to moderating rising prices and helping the marginalized in society, the findings were quite consistent with what we found in the 2011 QOL Survey. Then, in 2011, the top five areas that Singaporeans agreed most on about the role of the government were "The government should do more to address the needs of an ageing population" (still ranked 1st in 2016), "The government should provide more resources for the healthcare needs of the population" (ranked 5th in 2016), "The government should do more to improve the public transport system" (ranked 4th in 2016), "The government should provide more resources for the education needs of the population" (ranked 9th in 2016) and "The government should ensure that policing and law enforcement are effectively carried out" (ranked 6th in 2016).

The findings about how Singaporeans viewed the bottom five areas of government involvement were also quite consistent with what Tambyah and Tan (2013) found in the 2011 QOL Survey. The overlap was in three areas in which Singaporeans wanted minimal government involvement (for 2011): "The government should restrict the inflow of foreign workforce to protect domestic people's interests" (ranked 19th of 20 in 2016), "The government should provide more resources for the military and defense" (ranked 17th in 2016), "The government should provide more resources for the culture and the arts" (ranked 18th in 2016). In 2016, the two new areas of "The government should do more to provide more resources for leisure and recreational facilities" and "The government is responsible for my overall quality of life" were ranked 16th and 20th, respectively.

The areas of concern as noted in the 2016 QOL Survey with regard to the ageing population, rising prices and healthcare overlapped with the results of the Perceptions of Governance Survey (Tan 2015). The issues that most influenced how Singaporeans voted during the 2015 General Election were cost of living (64.6 percent), housing affordability (43.2 percent), healthcare affordability (42 percent), meeting retirement needs (37.2 percent) and government transparency and

Table 8.12 Views on the role of the government

Statements	Strongly disagree 1	Disagree 2	Neither agree nor disagree 3	Agree 4	Strongly agree 5	Mean (rank)
	%	%	%	%	%	
1. The government should restrict the inflow of foreign workforce to protect domestic people's interests.	1.1	7.6	25.8	48.4	17.1	3.73 (19)
2. The government should do more to protect the environment.	0.1	0.7	13.9	66.9	18.5	4.03 (13)
3. The government should provide more resources for the healthcare needs of the population.	0	0.7	7.9	62.7	28.7	**4.19 (5)**
4. The government should ensure that policing and law enforcement are effectively carried out.	0	0.4	7.7	65.7	26.2	4.18 (6)
5. The government should provide more resources for the education needs of the population.	0	0.8	10.3	62.7	26.1	4.14 (9)
6. The government should provide more resources for the military and defense.	0.9	3.6	21.8	58.5	15.2	3.83 (17)
7. The government should do more to address the needs of an ageing population	0	0.3	6.7	57.0	36.1	**4.29 (1)**
8. The government should do more to improve the public transport system.	0	0.8	7.8	58.6	32.8	**4.23 (4)**
9. The government should do more to improve the public services infrastructure.	0	0.9	12.2	62.7	24.2	4.10 (10)
10. The government should provide more resources for the culture and the arts.	0.1	2.8	26.3	56.5	14.3	3.82 (18)
11. The government should do more to better manage the bureaucracy and red tape (e.g., rules and regulations).	0.1	0.8	21.9	61.8	15.4	3.92 (15)
12. The government should do more to provide more resources for leisure and recreational facilities.	0.1	1.9	21.2	62.5	14.3	3.89 (16)
13. The government should do more to protect consumers against business malpractices.	0.1	0.2	12.4	65.6	21.8	4.09 (11)

(Continued)

Table 8.12 (Continued)

Statements	Strongly disagree 1	Disagree 2	Neither agree nor disagree 3	Agree 4	Strongly agree 5	Mean (rank)
	%	%	%	%	%	
14. The government should do more to moderate rising prices.	0.4	0.9	8.3	53.3	37.1	**4.26** **(2)**
15. The government should do more to provide career opportunities.	0.1	0.6	9.6	61.3	28.4	4.17 (7)
16. The government should do more to help the marginalised in society (e.g. handicapped, low-income households).	0	0.1	8.1	57.2	34.6	**4.26** **(2)**
17. The government should do more to improve the general quality of life for the citizens.	0	0.3	9.0	64.7	25.9	4.16 (8)
18. The government should do more to help preserve the Singapore culture and identity.	0	0.7	13.3	63.7	22.3	4.08 (12)
19. The government should emphasize national education to encourage patriotism.	0.3	2.0	16.1	63.7	17.8	3.97 (14)
20. The government is responsible for my overall quality of life.	1.1	8.3	25.7	54.0	11.0	3.65 (20)

Note: Percentages may not add up to 100 due to rounding errors.

Bold figures indicate the top five roles of the government.

accountability (35.1 percent). Tan (2015) referred to this focus on bread and butter issues as the "survival ideology" of Singaporeans, noting that this long-standing phenomenon now had a higher material baseline. Koh (2015) also observed in the 2015 IPS Post-election Survey that economic issues (such as the amount of government help to the needy and the cost of living) outranked political ideals (such as the need for checks and balances and diverse views in Parliament).

To examine how these views are correlated with Singaporeans' satisfaction with overall quality of life in Singapore, we conducted a regression analysis, using the responses to the 20 statements as independent variables and the Satisfaction with Overall Quality of Life in Singapore as the dependent variable. Table 8.13 shows the results of those statements that were significant in the regression analysis ($R^2 = 0.121$, F value = 10.242, $p<.000$).

Table 8.13 Impact of the role of government on satisfaction with overall quality of life in Singapore

Dependent variable: satisfaction with overall quality of life in Singapore	Unstandardized coefficients	Significance
The government should emphasize national education to encourage patriotism.	0.195	0.000
The government should provide more resources for the military and defense.	0.168	0.000
The government should ensure that policing and law enforcement are effectively carried out.	0.131	0.005
The government should provide more resources for the culture and the arts.	0.096	0.004
The government should do more to moderate rising prices.	−0.142	0.000
The government should do more to help preserve the Singapore culture and identity.	−0.120	0.008
The government should restrict the inflow of foreigners to protect the interests of locals.	−0.107	0.000

Note: Only statements that were significant in the regression analysis were shown in this table.

Table 8.13 shows that four areas (in order of their impact) are positively influenced by the role of the government:

1   Emphasize national education to encourage patriotism (ranked 14th).
2   Provide more resources for the military and defense (ranked 17th).
3   Ensure policing and law enforcement are effectively carried out (ranked 6th).
4   Provide more resources for the culture and arts (ranked 18th).

For the positive impact items, the respondents wanted more governmental involvement in these areas, as they felt this would have a positive impact on their satisfaction with overall quality of life in Singapore. Item 1 was about patriotism which the government may be able to develop at the national level. Items 2 and 3 were about the role of government in enforcing rules and regulations, and item 4 was about providing resources to improve the wellbeing of Singaporeans in the culture and arts.

Three areas were negatively influenced by the role of the government:

1   Moderate rising prices (ranked 2nd).
2   Help preserve Singapore culture and identity (ranked 12th).
3   Restrict the inflow of foreigners (ranked 19th).

For the negative impact items, the respondents felt that more governmental involvement in these areas would have a negative impact on their satisfaction with the overall quality of life in Singapore or that governmental action would be perceived as negative. This may imply that Singaporeans prefer less governmental involvement or interference in these areas, as these interventions may seem to be counterproductive. For item 2, Singaporeans may want more citizen participation in improving the quality of life and the preservation of the Singapore culture and identity.

We noted that the roles that had a positive impact were not necessarily the top-ranked roles that respondents wanted the government to be more involved in. Except for the 6th-ranked role about policing and law enforcement, the other three roles were low-ranked at 14th, 17th and 18th. Similarly, for the roles that had a negative impact, not all of them were the lowest-ranked roles, except for restricting the flow of foreigners (ranked 19th). In fact, the moderation of rising prices was s2nd-ranked, and the preservation of Singapore culture and identity was around the middle of the ranks at the 12th position. Thus, what respondents wanted the government to do may not be areas where there would be an impact (whether positive or negative) on their wellbeing, or they may be resigned to think that the efforts by the government would not be effective.

To examine whether these seven roles of government with significant positive or negative impact have any demographic implications, we did analyses of variances (ANOVA) across age, education, gender, household income and marital status (Tables 8.14 and 8.15). GR1 to GR4 correspond to the four positive impact items and GR5 to GR7 correspond to the three negative impact items.

As shown in Table 8.14, for the positive impact items GR1 to GR4, differences due to gender, marital status, age, education and household income exist. For GR1 (emphasize national education to encourage patriotism), Singaporeans in the youngest age group (15 to 24 years) felt least strongly about this role, while those aged between 45 to 64 years felt most strongly about it. Married Singaporeans and those with medium levels of education felt more strongly about this role than single Singaporeans and those with low or high levels of education. For GR2 (provide more resources for the military and defense), Singaporeans with medium levels of education felt most strongly about this role while those with high levels of education felt the least strongly. Females and married Singaporeans felt more strongly about this role than males and single Singaporeans. As for GR3 (ensure policing and law enforcement are effectively carried out), Singaporeans with high levels of education and income had the strongest sentiments, while those with low levels of education and income felt the least strongly about this role. For GR4 (provide more resources for culture and arts), those who were 35 to 44 years old felt the least strongly about this role versus those who were younger (15 to 24 years), who felt most strongly about this role. Females felt more strongly about this role than males.

As shown in Table 8.15, for the negative impact items GR5 to GR7, differences due to gender, marital status, age, education and household income exist. For GR5 (moderate rising prices), those 65 years and above felt most strongly about this role, while those aged 24 years and below felt the least strongly. For GR6 (help preserve Singapore culture and identity), again, only those with

Table 8.14 Sources of individual differences for the role of the government (positive impact)

Demographics	GR1	GR2	GR3	GR4
Age				
• 15–24	**3.79**	3.77	4.16	**3.92**
• 25–34	3.94	3.78	4.15	3.86
• 35–44	3.98	3.84	4.19	**3.72**
• 45–54	**4.03**	3.89	4.19	3.81
• 55–64	**4.03**	3.83	4.21	3.80
• 65 and above	4.01	3.92	4.15	3.84
• F-stats	**4.611**	1.451	.514	**2.237**
• p<	**.000**	.203	.766	**.048**
Education				
• Low	3.98	3.81	**4.12**	3.86
• Medium	**4.00**	**3.89**	4.16	3.83
• High	**3.90**	**3.73**	**4.24**	3.78
• F-stats	**3.326**	**6.915**	**3.666**	1.125
• p<	**.036**	**.001**	**.026**	.325
Gender				
• Male	3.95	**3.78**	4.15	**3.78**
• Female	3.99	**3.89**	4.20	**3.86**
• F-Stats	1.553	**8.830**	2.482	**5.052**
• p<	.213	**.003**	.115	**.025**
Household income[1]				
• Low	4.02	3.92	**4.12**	3.81
• Medium-low	3.98	3.82	4.25	3.81
• Medium-high	4.05	3.82	4.25	3.79
• High	3.83	3.71	**4.27**	3.73
• F-stats	1.909	1.878	**3.721**	0.914
• p<	.127	.132	**.011**	.339
Marital status				
• Single	**3.82**	3.74	4.14	3.84
• Married	**4.02**	3.85	4.19	3.80
• F-stats	**25.599**	**6.713**	1.643	0.762
• p<	**.000**	**.010**	.200	.383

1 Only for the 941 respondents who disclosed household income.

Bold figures indicate significance.

Table 8.15 Sources of individual differences for the role of the government (negative impact)

Demographics	GR5	GR6	GR7
Age			
• 15–24	**4.13**	4.05	**3.53**
• 25–34	4.27	4.14	**3.79**
• 35–44	4.29	4.08	3.72
• 45–54	4.28	4.09	3.78
• 55–64	4.27	4.10	3.78
• 65 and above	**4.30**	3.98	3.74
• F-stats	**4.695**	1.773	**3.093**
• p<	**.030**	.115	**.009**
Education			
• Low	4.26	**3.95**	**3.91**
• Medium	4.26	**4.13**	3.75
• High	4.26	4.04	**3.58**
• F-stats	0.004	**8.471**	**10.888**
• p<	.948	**.000**	**.000**
Gender			
• Male	4.24	4.06	**3.67**
• Female	4.28	4.09	**3.78**
• F-stats	1.012	.697	**6.992**
• p<	.315	.404	**.008**
Household income[1]			
• Low	4.31	4.11	**3.84**
• Medium-low	4.28	4.13	3.72
• Medium-high	4.31	4.16	3.59
• High	4.13	4.00	**3.38**
• F-stats	1.464	1.235	**7.172**
• p<	.223	.296	**.000**
Marital status			
• Single	4.23	4.04	**3.65**
• Married	4.27	4.08	**3.75**
• F-stats	1.174	1.248	**4.471**
• p<	.279	.264	**.035**

1 Only for the 941 respondents who disclosed household income.

Bold figures indicate significance.

medium levels of education felt more strongly about this role than those with low levels of education. For GR7 (restrict the inflow of foreigners), youngest Singaporeans (15 to 24 years old) felt least strongly about this role of government than young adult Singaporeans (25 to 34 years old), who had the strongest sentiments. Other demographic groups who felt more strongly about this role were the females, the married Singaporeans and those with low levels of education and incomes.

Conclusion

There was an improvement in the ratings for satisfaction with democratic rights from 2006 to 2011, but they have declined from 2011 to 2016. As noted in the findings, Singaporeans were not satisfied with their right to criticise the government, freedom of speech and to gather and demonstrate. From the demographic analyses, there were distinct segments of disgruntled citizens. Singles with medium levels of education and aged 25 to 35 years were most dissatisfied with their right to criticise the government and freedom of speech. Males were also unhappy about freedom of speech.

This enduring dissatisfaction that has been observed in the three surveys over the last ten years was not surprising given the Singapore government's reputation in political freedom. The Singapore government has been described as generally intolerant of criticism (e.g., George 2000, 2017). It curbs free speech through media control, fines, lawsuits and harassment of activists. Citizens are allowed to gather and demonstrate only at one designated spot (i.e., Speakers' Corner in Hong Lim Park), with many rules and regulations on what constitutes a legal assembly (see Human Rights Watch website). The unhappiness about such restrictions was most apparent in citizens aged 55 to 64 years, who were frustrated about their right to gather and demonstrate.

For the views on politics, although there was an improvement in the perceptions of the empathy and integrity of government officials, there were some naysayers among males who were 25 to 34 years of age with medium levels of education and with low or medium-low incomes. The perceptions of the efficacy of voting and the empowerment of voters were less favorable. There was also more doubt and ambivalence for these two areas of perception. From the demographic analyses for the efficacy of voting, citizens who were 25 to 35 years of age and with low levels of education and incomes were the most skeptical. For the empowerment of voters, males who were 25 to 35 years of age and with medium levels of education and low incomes felt the most disempowered. There was some convergence about which demographic groups were most disenfranchised (e.g., age, gender, education and income).

All these perceptions and views about politics have an impact on satisfaction with the overall quality of life in Singapore, except for corruption. As mentioned in Chapter 1, Singapore's anticorruption record has been good. Respondents generally believed that corruption was not a major problem. Thus, it did not have an impact on their satisfaction with the overall quality of life in Singapore.

However, the more nuanced perceptions and views about other aspects of politics mattered, including those related to democratic rights. Government officials have to move on to cultivating other positive perceptions of empathy and integrity, beyond being free from corruption.

Singaporeans wanted the government to allocate more resources to (1) addressing the needs of the ageing population, (2) moderating rising prices, (3) helping the marginalized in society, (4) improving the public transport system and (5) providing more resources for the healthcare needs of the population. For the role of the government, there were many varied demographic effects depending on the individual areas of priority. Generally, females, married people and those with medium levels of education appeared to be more security-conscious and ethnocentric in their concerns, and wanted more government spending and intervention in the areas of national education, the military and defense, and locals-first policies. Those with high incomes tended to be less ethnocentric but wanted more policing and law enforcement (similar to those with high levels of education). The young people (15–24 years) cared more about the culture and the arts and less about national education (a concern for the 45- to 54-year and 55- to 64-year age groups), the moderation of prices (a concern for the 65 years and above group) and locals-first policies. The 25- to 34-year age group was more concerned about locals-first policies, probably because they were the most affected by the competition for jobs and opportunities.

Whether the Singapore government is responsible for the happiness of its citizens is an interesting policy issue given the prominence of the ruling party (the People's Action Party) and its perceived largely paternalistic view of its role in ensuring the best for Singaporeans. In his analysis of Singapore and its model of democracy, Kampfner (2009) suggested that Singaporeans were not prepared to forgo their material comforts for a greater degree of freedom (e.g., freedom of speech and political freedom). As previously noted, levels of political participation remained low, although voters have been increasingly accessing the Internet and social media for political content and expression of views for the past two General Elections in 2011 and 2015. It remains to be seen whether citizens will take on a more active role in political participation (both online and offline) and in nurturing their internal and external political efficacy.

References

Bahry, D., and Silver, B. (1990), 'Soviet citizen participation on the eve of democratization', *American Political Science Review*, 84(3), 821–848.

Barnes, S., Farah, B. and Heunks, F. (1979), 'Personal dissatisfaction', in *Political action: Mass participation in five western democracies*, edited by S. Barnes, M. Kaase, et al., Beverly Hills, CA, USA: Sage, 381–408

Boelhouwer, J., and van Campen, C. (2013), 'Steering towards happiness in the Netherlands', *Social Indicators Research*, 114, 59–72.

Bok, D. (2010), *The politics of happiness*, Princeton, NJ, USA: Princeton University Press.

Flavin, P., and Keane, M. (2012), 'Life satisfaction and political participation: Evidence from the United States', *Journal of Happiness Studies*, 13(1), 63–78.

George, C. (2000), *Singapore: The air-conditioned nation*, Singapore: Landmark Books. www.airconditionednation.com/2015/07/05/free-speech/ (accessed November 29, 2017).

George C. (2017), *Singapore, incomplete: Reflections on a first world nation's arrested political development*, Singapore: Woodsville News.

Human Rights Watch www.hrw.org/world-report/2017/country-chapters/singapore (accessed November 29, 2017).

Institute of Policy Studies. The 2010 IPS Survey (Survey on Political Traits and Media Use). http://lkyspp2.nus.edu.sg/ips/wp-content/uploads/sites/2/2013/07/Media-Survey-Report_230511.pdf (accessed 28 November 2017).

Kampfner, J. (2009), *Freedom for sale: How we made money and lost our liberty*, London, UK: Simon & Schuster.

Koh, G. (2015), 'POPS (8) IPS Post-Election Survey 2015', presentation at the IPS Post-election Conference 2015, November 4, 2015. http://lkyspp2.nus.edu.sg/ips/wp-content/uploads/sites/2/2015/10/POPS-8_GE2015_061115_web-Final.pdf (accessed November 28, 2017).

Oishi, S., Diener, E., and Lucas, R.E. (2007), 'The optimal level of well-being: Can we be too happy?', *Perspectives on Psychological Science*, 2, 346–360.

Pacheco, G., and Lange, T. (2010), 'Political participation and life satisfaction: A cross-European analysis', *International Journal of Social Economics*, 37(10), 686–702.

Pirralha, A. (2017), 'Political participation and wellbeing in the Netherlands: Exploring the causal links', *Applied Research in Quality of Life*, 12, 327–341.

Putnam, R. (2000), *Bowling alone: The collapse and revival of American community*, New York, NY, USA: Simon & Schuster.

Soon, C. (2015), 'Study on Internet and media use during general election 2015', presentation at the IPS Post-Election Conference 2015, November 4, 2015. http://lkyspp2.nus.edu.sg/ips/wp-content/uploads/sites/2/2015/10/S1_Carol-Soon_PEC_Media-Panel_041115.pdf (accessed December 5, 2017).

Tambyah, S.K., and Tan, S.J. (2013), *Happiness and wellbeing: The Singaporean experience*, London, UK: Routledge.

Tambyah, S.K., Tan, S.J., and Kau, A.K. (2010), *The wellbeing of Singaporeans: Values, lifestyles, satisfaction and quality of life*, Singapore: World Scientific Publishing.

Tan, E.S. (2015), 'Explaining the GE2015 outcomes: Insights from the perceptions of governance survey', presentation at the IPS Post-Election Conference 2015, November 4, 2015. http://lkyspp2.nus.edu.sg/ips/wp-content/uploads/sites/2/2015/10/S2_ES_Explaining-the-GE2015-outcomes-041115_Web.pdf (accessed December 5, 2017).

Teorell, J. (2006), 'Political participation and three theories of democracy: A research inventory and agenda', *European Journal of Political Research*, 45, 787–810.

Veenhoven, R. (1988), 'The utility of happiness', *Social Indicators Research*, 20(4), 333–354.

Verba, S., and Nie, N. (1972), *Participation in America*, New York, NY, USA: Harper & Row.

Weitz-Shapiro, R., and Winters, M.S. (2011), 'The link between voting and life satisfaction in Latin America', *Latin American Politics and Society*, 53(4), 101–126.

9 Conclusion

In this concluding chapter, we synthesize the key findings of the 2016 QOL Survey and discuss how these findings support one another to provide a holistic perspective of happiness and wellbeing in Singapore. As seen in the earlier chapters, we have covered a wide range of topics on happiness and wellbeing, including satisfaction with life domains and living in Singapore, happiness, enjoyment, achievement, control, purpose, psychological flourishing, the relationship between income and happiness, economic wellbeing, personal values, value orientations, trust and social capital, satisfaction with democratic rights, views on politics, and the role of the government. We conducted demographic analyses and showed how perceptions of subjective wellbeing may vary across age, education, gender, monthly household income and marital status. Where applicable, we made longitudinal comparisons of the 2016 QOL Survey data with previous datasets from the 2011 QOL Survey (Tambyah and Tan 2013), the 2006 AsiaBarometer Survey (Tambyah et al. 2010), the 2001 survey (Kau et al. 2004) and the 1996 Survey (Kau et al. 1998), and noted the variations and trends over the years. In addition, we examined the impact of personal values, trust, satisfaction with democratic rights, views on politics and the role of the government on satisfaction indicators (satisfaction with life, the overall quality of life and the overall quality of life in Singapore) and wellbeing indicators (happiness, enjoyment, achievement, control and purpose). In the sections to follow, we will begin with a note on the economic, social and political climate of the 2016 QOL Survey, followed by the discussion on the multifaceted aspects of wellbeing, the effects of demographics, the income and happiness debate and what matters for the satisfaction and wellbeing of Singaporeans. We end the chapter with directives for future research.

The economic, social and political climate of the 2016 QOL Survey

For the 2011 QOL Survey (results were reported in Tambyah and Tan 2013), we noted that Singapore was recovering well from the turbulent years of the late 2000s. The economy grew at 4.9 percent in 2011, and the employment rate for the resident population improved to 2.1 percent. However, there were also inflationary pressures and increasing costs of living. Inflationary pressures eased in 2016 (inflation rate of –0.5 percent) and 2017 (inflation rate of 0.4 percent), and the official resident unemployment rate in 2017 was low at 2.1 percent (similar to 2011).

The 2011 QOL Survey was conducted in June and July 2011, a month after what has been described as a watershed General Election for Singapore (Welsh 2011). The ruling political party, the People's Action Party (PAP), regained power in the Parliament but garnered the lowest percentage of votes (60.14 percent) since Singapore's independence in 1965. For the first time, a Group Representative Constituency, which is a mega conglomeration of five constituencies, was won by an alternative political party, the Workers Party. The 2016 QOL Survey was conducted during November 2016 to February 2017. The most recent election was the 2015 General Election. The PAP capitalized on the nationalistic pride kindled by Singapore's Jubilee Year and the passing of Singapore's first Prime Minister, Mr. Lee Kuan Yew and rebounded with 69.86 percent of the popular vote (the highest since 2001's victory of 75.3 percent).

Multifaceted aspects of wellbeing

Satisfaction indicators

The 2016 QOL Survey showed that Singaporeans were generally satisfied with their lives in general but less so with living in Singapore, although the satisfaction with the latter slightly improved. In terms of satisfaction with life domains (Chapter 2), across the four surveys conducted in 1996, 2001, 2011 and 2016, Singaporeans were most satisfied with their familial relationships, although satisfaction with marriage/romantic relationships was lower in 2016. Generally, Singaporeans continued to do well in the life domains of social wellbeing and family life. Consistently, in 2011 and 2016, Singaporeans were most dissatisfied with their household income and level of education. In terms of satisfaction with the overall quality of life, Singaporeans' rating on this item registered a gradual increase between the years 1996 to 2011, but it dipped slightly in 2016 (mean of 4.72). Singaporeans' satisfaction with the overall quality of life in Singapore registered an increase (mean of 4.66), thus reversing the declining trend since 2001. However, from the means, we noted that Singaporeans were still more satisfied with their overall quality of life than with their overall quality of life in Singapore.

Similar to 1996, 2001, 2006 and 2011, in 2016, the top areas in which Singaporeans were the most satisfied with living in Singapore were related to the level of safety and security, the availability of public services, the quality of law enforcement and education, and the convenience of public transport. Consistently, the affordability issues (for cars and properties) were the top main grouses of Singaporeans in the surveys of 1996, 2001 and 2011.

Age and education were the main driving forces accounting for four out of five top life domains that Singaporeans were satisfied with, followed by marital status (three out of five domains). Gender and household income were less influential (accounting for two out of five domains). Individual differences due to age and education were repeated for the top five domains that Singaporeans were dissatisfied with, followed by marital status and household income (accounting for three out of five domains), while gender had no impact.

Wellbeing indicators

Over the past ten years (2006–2016), Singaporeans have become less happy, enjoyed life less and have felt a decreased sense of achievement (Chapter 3). For the 2016 QOL Survey, most Singaporeans felt they had some control over their lives and a sense of purpose in life. It remains to be seen how the control and purpose indexes will change over time, together with the movements in the Happiness, Enjoyment and Achievement Indexes.

Education and household income had the most impact on Singaporeans' self- assessment of their happiness, enjoyment, achievement, control and purpose, while gender did not make any difference. Marital status was the next most impactful demographic variable, affecting Singaporeans' self-assessment of achievement, control and purpose. Age made a difference only when Singaporeans were self-assessing their achievements.

Using Diener and Biswas-Diener's (2008) 12-item Psychological Flourishing Scale, we found that Singaporeans had declined in their psychological flourishing over the five years from 2011 to 2016. Demographically, education, gender, household income, and marital status contributed to differences in Singaporeans' assessment of their state of psychological flourishing.

The effect of demographics on satisfaction and wellbeing

For the 2016 QOL Survey, we noted sources of individual differences for different demographic groups for the various satisfaction and wellbeing indicators. The gender effect seemed to be less pronounced, and marital status had some impact (mainly for life domains and Singaporeans' self-assessment of achievement, control and purpose). Age, education and income contributed to more differentiation. Age and education were more important for satisfaction outcomes, while education and household income had the most impact on Singaporeans' wellbeing indicators, such as happiness, enjoyment, achievement, control and purpose. Age made a difference only for Singaporeans' sense of achievement. While these sources of individual differences provided additional insights, care should be taken in interpreting some of the results as the correlations were generally small (which is common in social sciences studies of this nature).

Income, happiness and economic wellbeing

One demographic that was identified for more in-depth analysis for this book was household income. Household income had some impact on Singaporeans' satisfaction indicators (Chapter 2). Generally, respondents with higher incomes also had higher means on the wellbeing indicators of happiness, enjoyment, achievement, control and purpose (Chapter 3). In Chapter 4, we noted the upward trending patterns correlating household income with the satisfaction and wellbeing indicators. However, those with the highest household incomes might not be the happiest or most satisfied.

In terms of economic wellbeing, our analyses confirmed that satisfaction with household income (i.e., financial satisfaction) and satisfaction with standard of living were positively associated with the wellbeing indicators. Singaporeans' responses to the four evaluative questions measuring economic wellbeing showed that, in terms of buying items for basic needs, meeting obligatory payments and doing things they want to do, Singaporeans were economically comfortable. However, when it comes to making a major purchase like a car or a home appliance or paying for significant home repairs, the majority of Singaporeans (55.5 percent) were unable to do so. We also noted that Singaporeans were most dissatisfied with the affordability of cars, and it was the lowest-ranked (25th) aspect of living in Singapore (Chapter 2).

As observed in our QOL Surveys over the years, Singaporeans have always been concerned about their economic wellbeing. As mentioned earlier, it appeared that more financial resources were needed to provide opportunities for happiness, enjoyment and achievement, control and purpose. The ability to meet this need would be more difficult for those with lower levels of household income.

Values and wellbeing

Values, as enduring systems of beliefs and preferences, have an impact on the wellbeing of Singaporeans. There were no significant shifts in value importance over the past two decades (1996–2016) as Singaporeans consistently rated Self-respect, Security, Warm Relationships with Others and Sense of Belonging as values of high importance. In 2016, Sense of Belonging, Fun and Enjoyment, and Self-fulfillment were the three values which had the most significant influence on Singaporeans' subjective wellbeing. Sense of Belonging had a positive influence on Singaporeans' Happiness, Enjoyment, Achievement, and Purpose. Fun and Enjoyment had a positive impact on Enjoyment, Achievement and Control, while Self-fulfillment had a positive influence on Achievement, Control and Purpose.

When examining the impact of LOV on subjective wellbeing in terms of life satisfaction, Sense of Belonging and Warm Relationships with Others were the two most important values that had a positive influence on Singaporeans' satisfaction with life, satisfaction with overall quality of life, and satisfaction with overall quality of life in Singapore. Security positively influenced only Singaporeans' satisfaction with overall quality of life in Singapore, while Sense of Accomplishment negatively influenced only Singaporeans' satisfaction with life. The values of Self-respect, Self-fulfillment and Excitement had no significant roles to play on Singaporeans' life satisfaction.

Thus, it seems that, in order to enhance Singaporeans' subjective wellbeing, it would be good to have a well-rounded approach to life in terms of nurturing a sense of belonging (to family, friends and the larger community), to have some fun and enjoyment (to relieve the stresses of everyday life) and to cultivate self-fulfillment (a sense of meaning and purpose in what we do).

In terms of Schwartz's four Higher Order Values, Singaporeans placed a high priority on Self-transcendence (which includes the basic values of universalism and benevolence) and Conservation (which includes the basic values of conformity, tradition and security) but a lower priority on Openness (which includes the basic values of stimulation, self-direction and hedonism) and Self-enhancement (which includes the basic values of achievement and power). Conservation was the most important factor having a positive impact on Singaporeans' happiness, enjoyment, achievement and control. Self-transcendence was the only value that had a positive impact on Singaporeans' control and purpose. Openness had a positive impact on Singaporeans' enjoyment, while Self-enhancement had a negative impact.

In terms of life satisfaction, Conservation was the most important value with a positive influence on Singaporeans' satisfaction with life, satisfaction with overall quality of life, and satisfaction with overall quality of life in Singapore. Self-transcendence had a positive influence on Singaporeans' satisfaction with overall quality of life and satisfaction with overall quality of life in Singapore, while Openness had a negative influence only on Singaporeans' satisfaction with overall quality of life in Singapore. Self-enhancement had no significant influences over Singaporeans' life satisfaction. Our results showed that Singaporeans' subjective wellbeing (in terms of wellbeing or satisfaction indicators) were driven mostly by values such as conformity, tradition, and security rather than by values such as achievement and power.

Clusters of Singaporeans

In 2016, we had five clusters of Singaporeans as follows: Pro-Social Family Oriented, Materialistic Family Oriented, Traditional Entrepreneurs, Status Conscious and Dreamers. The revision in the number and composition of the clusters over the years (eight clusters in 2001 and six clusters in 2011) could be partly attributed to the changes in the compositions of the value orientations, shifts in the scores that respondents gave to each value item and changes in the demographics of the respondents. Despite the revision in the number of clusters over the years, family-oriented clusters still featured prominently in the clustering of Singaporeans. This underscores the importance Singaporeans placed on family values, as found in our past QOL surveys.

Singaporeans' strong emphasis on family values and traditionalism placed Singapore on the Traditional values dimension of the World Values Survey's analysis of cultural variation in the world. The focus of Singaporeans on materialism, eco-orientation and entrepreneurial spirit would also fit in with the Survival values dimension. According to the World Values Survey analysis, these two dimensions implied that Singaporeans tended to be nationalistic with a relatively ethnocentric outlook and low levels of trust and tolerance. This low level of trust also came to light when we examined trust in Chapter 7.

Trust and wellbeing

We found that generalized trust was not high among Singaporeans. Overall, Singaporeans' responses to the three trust questions revealed that they were wary of others, did not really think others could be helpful but were willing to concede that most people would try to be fair. Comparing the results of the 2016 QOL Survey and those from the 2009 ASEAN Barometer Survey, Singaporeans' trust instincts did not seem to have improved over the years. The climate for generalized trust could be improved in Singapore. This would be important as our analyses showed that generalized trust had a significant and positive impact on happiness, health and all three measures of life satisfaction.

It is thus imperative that Singaporeans at all levels of society and the institutions and organizations that they are a part of continue to develop and deepen the trust among the individuals and communities who live and work in Singapore. This would not be easy given the increasing heterogeneity of the Singapore Resident population and the perceived competition for opportunities and resources.

Rights, politics and role of the government and wellbeing

In terms of the impact of satisfaction with democratic rights on the satisfaction with the overall quality of life in Singapore, all the rights have a positive impact except for the right to gather and demonstrate. Having a duty to vote, a good understanding of politics and the efficacy of their votes have a positive impact on Singaporeans' satisfaction with the overall quality of life in Singapore. On the other hand, there was a negative impact on Singaporeans' satisfaction with overall quality of life in Singapore when voters felt they could not influence government policy or actions and when government officials do not care about or pay attention to the citizens. Our results implied that there was a need to enhance the internal and external political efficacy of Singaporeans so that they can better understand the political system and the role they play in it. Although Singaporeans were often viewed as politically apathetic, there were indications that voters would like to have accountability, transparency and political freedom.

Singaporeans wanted the government to step up in the top five areas of (1) addressing the needs of the ageing population, (2) moderating rising prices, (3) helping the marginalized in society, (4) improving the public transport system and (5) providing more resources for the healthcare needs of the population.

That the government should do more to address the needs of an ageing population was also the most important priority for government spending in 2011. Numerous initiatives have been implemented and more are being developed to promote active ageing, ageing in place and the integration of caregiving in the larger community, support for caregivers and participation in the workforce for older workers. More funds have also been invested in the strengthening of the infrastructure (e.g., nursing homes, hospices, community hospitals and enhanced accessibility around the housing estates) and for the training of more healthcare professionals. A related issue is government spending on healthcare, which was ranked 5th in 2016 and 2nd in 2011. Healthcare had been a hot-button issue during the 2011 and 2015 General Elections. Measures to provide for the healthcare needs of the Pioneer Generation and more subsidies for lower-income Singaporeans were well received and helped to mitigate some of the fears about rising medical costs.

The moderation of rising prices (which is related to economic wellbeing) was the second-ranked priority for government intervention. Various cooling measures for the housing market and restrictions on ownership have been in place since 2011. However, the effect on prices has been moderate. Attempts to lower car prices within the current Certificate of Entitlement bidding system for the rights to car ownership have not been sustainable. The government has been pushing its vision for a "car-lite Singapore." However, concerns with the safely and reliability of the public transport system (4th-ranked priority) had stalled some of the progress made thus far.

Future research directives

This book is part of our continuing efforts to measure the happiness and wellbeing of Singaporeans through the years. There are now at least four nationally representative datasets (survey data collected in 1996, 2001, 2011 and 2016/2017 for the 2016 QOL Survey) over 20 years for satisfaction with life, life domains and living in Singapore, personal values and value orientations. For indicators of happiness, enjoyment, achievement and satisfaction with rights, there are also three nationally representative datasets (the 2006 AsiaBarometer Survey, the 2011 QOL Survey and the 2016 QOL Survey).

In successive waves of the QOL Surveys, we have tried to maintain a balance of measures in our questionnaires. In the 2016 QOL Survey, we introduced the Satisfaction with Life Scale, Schwartz's Portrait Value Questionnaire, and questions on control and purpose. The analyses and results obtained from these new measures were discussed in this book. For comparisons with past surveys, we kept the measures on personal values (List of Values), value orientations (with some modifications), satisfaction with democratic rights, views about politics and the role of the government (with some new additions). Economic wellbeing and psychological flourishing (which were first introduced in the 2011 QOL Survey) were also part of the 2016 QOL Survey. For future surveys, we will continue to refine the various measures currently used and introduce measures to account for new developments in the research on wellbeing and changes in the context of Singapore. Some possibilities include more measures on the eudaimonic aspects of wellbeing relating to engagement, meaning and purpose. We would like to include objective or perceptual measures of relative income to augment the analysis on the relationship between income and happiness. We would also consider incorporating measures on postmaterialistic values to enhance the analysis on values and wellbeing.

We have used cross-sectional surveys in the four QOL Surveys (1996, 2001, 2011 and 2016) to study changes in values and their influence on subjective wellbeing. These surveys drew representative samples of the Singapore citizen population using the same method at repeated times, allowing us to look at several snapshots of Singapore and to assess the degree of stability or change within the society. Our cross-sectional studies have an advantage over longitudinal studies in that they have built-in corrections for the changing composition of a sampling unit, and they do not require keeping track of the movements of mobile individuals.

Nevertheless, future research could also include the construction of a nationally representative sample of Singaporeans who could be tracked longitudinally for their values and life satisfaction. Findings from the longitudinal studies could then be compared with those of cross-sectional sequential studies for greater insights into the temporal stability of the values and life satisfaction of Singaporeans, particularly in examining the presence of cohort effects.

We reiterate our concern and call for more government and corporate funding and research support to sustain the research on happiness, quality of life and subjective wellbeing in the Singaporean context. While a common, composite index of the quality of life for Singaporeans is still not currently available, we noted that various universities (e.g., the Singapore University of Social Sciences) and research institutes (e.g., the Institute of Policy Studies) have conducted studies on the subjective wellbeing of Singaporeans and various key sociopolitical issues.

Concluding remarks

Singapore had its 50th Jubilee Year in 2015 with a yearlong SG50 celebration and with a mixture of aplomb and excitement, along with nostalgia and soul-searching. Along with the achievements of the past 50 years, Singapore also had its fair share of challenges. The nation has made tremendous economic progress, putting in place a very efficient infrastructure for business, industry and foreign investment. Singapore seemed to be materially prosperous with a high GDP per capita and a good standard of living. However, there were Singaporeans who were concerned about having enough to enjoy their lives and fulfill their dreams and aspirations beyond meeting the basic needs. Socially, the bonds of family and community have held up well, although they have been tested with the influx of foreigners in recent years and the rapid increase of the resident population. Social connectedness could provide the psychological benefits of social integration and displace the role of money as a source of status and self-worth (Richards 2016).

Singapore is in a good place, having attained many of the key requirements for an economically viable society and other aspects of living that contribute to happiness such as family, relationships and spiritual groundedness (Buettner 2010). What will Singapore be like when it is a hundred years old? Moving beyond our role as researchers, we, as citizens of Singapore, hope that Singaporeans will cultivate the right values, trust, openness and democratic processes that are necessary for a happy society. We also hope that Singapore as a society will grow and thrive in other aspects of wellbeing beyond economic prosperity and material abundance. As suggested by Crespo and Mesurado (2015), it is time to move on from happiness economics to flourishing economics.

References

Buettner, D. (2010), *Thrive: Finding happiness in the blue zones way*, Washington, DC, USA: National Geographic.

Crespo, R.F., and Mesurado, B. (2015), 'Happiness economics, eudaimonia and positive psychology: From happiness economics to flourishing economics', *Journal of Happiness Studies*, 16, 931–946.

Diener, E., and Biswas-Diener, R. (2008), *Happiness: Unlocking the mysteries of psychological wealth*, New York, NY, USA: Blackwell.

Kau, A.K., Jung, K., Tambyah, S.K., and Tan, S.J. (2004), *Understanding Singaporeans: Values, lifestyles, aspirations and consumption behaviors*, Singapore: World Scientific Publishing.

Kau, A.K., Tan, S.J., and Wirtz, J. (1998), *Seven faces of Singaporeans: Their values, aspirations and lifestyles*, Singapore: Prentice Hall.

Richards, L. (2016), 'For whom money matters less: Social connectedness as a resilience resource in the UK', *Social Indicators Research*, 125, 509–535.

Tambyah, S.K., and Tan, S.J. (2013), *Happiness and wellbeing: The Singaporean experience*, London, UK: Routledge.

Tambyah, S.K., Tan, S.J., and Kau, A.K. (2010), *The wellbeing of Singaporeans: Values, lifestyles, satisfaction and quality of life*, Singapore: World Scientific Publishing.

Welsh, B. (2011), Soul searching Singapore's 2011 General Election. *Asia Pacific Bulletin*, 118, June 23, 2011. http://myemail.constantcontact.com/Asia-Pacific-Bulletin-Soul-Searching-Singapore-s-2011-General-Election.html?soid=110215 7595489&aid=O-JQxC8XdkU#fblike (accessed January 20, 2018).

Index